Praise for <u>Changing Direction</u>:

"The essence of Lenore's distinctive methods, developed over many years, can be found in the pages of this excellent, clearly written book."

—Ang Lee, Director

"Lenore DeKoven says in her introduction to her book, <u>Changing Direction</u>, that 'everyone wants to be in show business'. Well I am, but I've never wanted to direct. After reading Lenore's book, I may reconsider my career choice."

—Edward Asner, Actor/Producer

"I was one of the many people who, over the years, asked Lenore to write her book, and finally she has. It's a thrill to read, as well as a reminder of her great gift—her deep understanding of drama, directing, actors, everyday life, and most importantly her wealth of experience and huge heart. I will draw from this every time I work."

—Kimberly Peirce, writer/director of <u>Boys Don't Cry</u>, <u>Stop-Loss</u>, student of Lenore

"Lenore DeKoven has written a great book for the director searching for practical advice on the techniques of directing actors. Her work as a teacher has already affected a generation of young filmmakers. One would be hard-pressed to find a more comprehensive and clear approach to working with actors."

—Bette Gordon, Director and Acting Chair of Film Division, School of the Arts, Columbia University

"This book is much needed on the shelves for students and individuals interested in directing actors for film and theatre. Very few books offer this approach with such specific and practical steps laid out in detail, step by step."

—Sheldon Schiffer, Georgia State University

852947

Photo by George Kunze

Lenore DeKoven has had a distinguished and varied career in film, theatre, and television. Her activity in the film industry has included executive positions in the talent and story departments of Hecht-Lancaster and Palomar Pictures. She was the managing director of the Roundabout Theatre Company in its earlier days as well as the producer of several off-Broadway productions. DeKoven was a member of the Theatre Arts Division faculty of UCLA, where she taught acting and directing on the undergraduate and graduate levels. She directed <u>The Miracle Worker</u> at Freud Playhouse before returning to New York in 1980, where she directed <u>Another World</u> for NBCTV. She is a member of the Directors Guild of America and the League of Professional Theatre Women and has directed many plays and staged readings in New York. From 1981 to 1988 she was on both the theatre and film faculties of NYU's Tisch School of the Arts. Since 1988 she has been a member of the directing actors faculty of the Graduate Film Division of Columbia University's School of the Arts. Since 1981 she has been artistic director of Our Workshop East, a development gym for actors, writers, and directors.

Changing Direction

A Practical Approach to Directing Actors in Film and Theatre

Lenore DeKoven

ELSEVIER

AMSTERDAM • BOSTON • HEIDELBERG • LONDON
NEW YORK • OXFORD • PARIS • SAN DIEGO
SAN FRANCISCO • SINGAPORE • SYDNEY • TOKYO
Focal Press is an imprint of Elsevier

Acquisitions Editor:	Elinor Actipis
Project Manager:	Dawnmarie Simpson
Developmental Editor:	Becky Golden-Harrell
Assistant Editor:	Robin Weston
Marketing Manager:	Christine Degon Veroulis
Cover Design:	Cate Barr

Front cover image "Winding road in Fall Black Hills, South Dakota" © Laurance B Aiuppy/Taxi/Getty Images, Inc.

Focal Press is an imprint of Elsevier
30 Corporate Drive, Suite 400, Burlington, MA 01803, USA
Linacre House, Jordan Hill, Oxford OX2 8DP, UK

Recognizing the importance of preserving what has been written, Elsevier prints its books on acid-free paper whenever possible.

Library of Congress Cataloging-in-Publication Data
DeKoven, Lenore.
   Changing direction : a practical approach to directing actors in film and theatre/Lenore DeKoven.
      p. cm.
   Includes index.
   ISBN-13: 978-0-240-80664-8 (pbk. : alk. paper)
   ISBN-10: 0-240-80664-6 (pbk. : alk. paper)
   1. Theater—Production and direction.   2. Motion pictures—Production and direction.
I. Title.
   PN2053.D44 2006
   792.02'33—dc22

2005029190

British Library Cataloguing-in-Publication Data
A catalogue record for this book is available from the British Library.

ISBN 13: 978-0-240-80664-8
ISBN 10: 0-240-80664-6

For information on all Focal Press publications
visit our website at www.books.elsevier.com

06   07   08   09   10   11   10   9   8   7   6   5   4   3   2   1

Printed in the United States of America

Contents

Foreword

I took Lenore DeKoven's acting/directing class when I was a graduate student in film at New York University and continued working with her in a private workshop for another 2 years. The essence of Lenore's distinctive methods, developed over many years, can be found in the pages of this excellent, clearly written book.

Taking Lenore's class is like working with a great director. And of course, directing is, in some ways, a form of teaching. A lot of directing involves intuition, which cannot be taught. But I learned a great deal not only from the things she taught me, but also from the way she taught them. Lenore begins with the basic idea that the relationship between the actor and the director is the most important element in filmmaking (as well as theatre, television, etc.). In her workshops, there are actors as well as directors. She teaches us not only how to direct an actor, but also how it feels to be an actor.

Lenore is a rigorous teacher, who makes her students go back to the beginning of the scene again and again, because the most important part of the scene is its starting point. She responds to her students eloquently, examining the performances in terms of the character's needs, because getting these needs right in the starting point is the key to the scene's dramatic development. Needs provide the basic dramatic design for the story and the framework for the collaboration between director and actor. Every main character has his or her own basic needs: achieving positive feelings (to get love, earn respect, prove one's worth, and so on) and getting rid of negative ones (guilt, insecurity, fear, and so on). And for each need, different actors may find the different actions that define their performance and bring the drama to life.

I was very flattered to find three of my films included in her list of recommended viewing at the end of the book: <u>Sense and</u>

Sensibility, The Ice Storm, and Brokeback Mountain. Whatever the finished result, there is something of what she taught me in the process of filmmaking. The most important thing I took away from her classes is how to figure out the subtext; her teaching contributed to the shaping of the performances in all three films. As each film was in a different genre, made under different circumstances with different types of actors and at different points of my career, her methods, which have become a habitual part of my working process, were used (and sometimes misused) in different ways.

In Sense and Sensibility, I was working with some of the most brilliant British actors. Based on their tradition, I found they often approached their characters from the outside in, using texture to show inner feeling, shaping their performances with nuances and gestures. The material was very literary, full of great lines, very verbal. In short, the challenge was to express sensibility working within a tradition of acting that is very much based on sense. How do you get performances that the audience can admire, but also feel moved by? One of the most difficult moments in the film came in the scene where Emma Thompson finds out that Hugh Grant is still available and loses control of her emotions. In this case, I settled on a very simple suggestion: I told Emma that I didn't want to see more than her profile. I knew right away that something great would come from this. Emma's heart reached out (her sensibility, the need to get love), even as her body resisted by turning away (her sense, the need to maintain propriety). The result was one of the most touching scenes in the film.

The Ice Storm deals with clueless characters that have no idea what they're doing. The fact that they are played by the best possible trained actors, who know exactly what they're doing, was one of the big challenges in making this film. My work with Kevin Kline is a good example of how I dealt with this—to identify the need and inner conflict that would drive his performance and then defeat it, to beat him down until he was clueless. A good example is the scene where Kevin's character tells his teenage daughter: "Go to bed by 10, and I mean it!" Working closely with Kevin, I had him repeat this line over and over again, wearing him down, until I got the feeling that the girl would ignore his orders and not go to bed by 10. Despite the way this sounds, I think Kevin really appreciated this kind of working relationship.

Unlike Sense and Sensibility, which reflects a verbal culture, Brokeback Mountain, my latest film, is about a nonverbal culture, based in the American west. From the original short story, the film inherited a sense of silence and space; the mood is elegiac and poetic rather than dramatic. Here, I still began by defining the characters' needs and conflicts. I worked carefully with the actors Jake Gyllenhall and Heath Ledger, setting up their starting point and developing the sense of space and time in their relationship with each other, within themselves, and between themselves and the landscape. The performances were mainly about body language, about rhythm and pauses, rather than speech; the action took place between the lines rather than on the lines.

Although it mimics life, I have found that drama in film is simpler and limited to a much smaller stage. That is why it's more effective to narrow down the motivations, to set up the needs in the most actable and most communicable way.

Of course, there's more to a director's job than dealing with acting. Even working with actors is not all about acting. Sometimes, it's less about performance than positioning, where the actors stand in the physical space of the scene. It's also about the way the actors look and their disposition. Finding actors who look right for the role can be a significant part in making a movie. Performances can also be shaped in the editing room, where the director acts with his or her scissors.

One of the director's biggest jobs, which also goes beyond acting, is that of creating a world for the characters to live in—the costumes, the physical setting, the historical details. The process of filmmaking also involves the director's "aura," the personality he or she projects when on set. Actors are not made of clay, but flesh and blood, with tempers and thoughts and wills of their own. You can't simply manipulate them; you must be able to invite them into your world, and they must feel inspired working within it. When this is not the case, the director's job can become very difficult.

No method is equal to the end result. In the end, it's all about how the audience responds to the finished play or film. The audience doesn't simply sit back and appreciate the acting; the audience is the actor. In <u>Brokeback Mountain</u>, for example, Heath Ledger's performance is so moving because he plays a repressed character, and so much of the performance happens between the lines. Such a performance makes the audience feel the emotions that his character cannot express. As Lenore sometimes puts it, if you feel sorry for yourself, nobody needs to feel sorry for you. The work of the director and actor is not about feeling emotions, but finding the actions that will allow the audience to feel the emotions.

Changing Direction is about more than just working with actors. The director must make himself or herself available to the entire creative and technical team. The work begins with knowing the subtext of the story and the basic needs that move the characters and create the conflict that drives the drama. This is the base that will allow you to be responsive to everyone who works on the film and to every situation that will arise over the entire filmmaking process.

I found my starting point in Lenore DeKoven's classes. I would like to thank her for giving me the confidence to navigate through all the changing directions of my career.

—Ang Lee
Director

Preface

For years now my students and workshop members have been begging me to write a book about my approach to directing actors and its vocabulary. "Give us lists," they've implored. "Write us a text of the course." I've successfully resisted their pleas until now, mainly because I suspected that one couldn't get a real sense of this material from reading a book. Behavior, which is the core of our work, is so involved with the visual. You have to *see* it to study it. To understand my approach you have to *do* it. To make it useful for yourself you have to make it part of your cells, get it into your bloodstream.

And then of course there was a certain unwillingness on my part to take on the challenge of attempting to write down on pages a process by which we might arrive at something so dynamic, ephemeral, flexible, constantly adjusting and changing as the re-creation of life. How does one painstakingly describe in prose the betraying twitch of a muscle, the revealing physical response to an emotion, or the unexpected reaction of a querulous actor? As I am more director than writer, the prospect of attempting to make my approach clear while adhering to my strong belief that shorter is better in most forms of communication, loomed ominous.

In addition there was another nagging thought that loitered in my consciousness as I contemplated the act of writing about directors and the direction of actors. How would I handle the issue of the pronoun used to refer to the director? For most of my adult life, I've been fighting the battle against sexism, particularly in the area of the entertainment industry. When I began to move from acting to directing, there were no female directors on Broadway, none shooting feature films, and none working in prime time television. Although there were female producers and writers, women were simply not hired as directors. Organizations such as Women in

Film (both in Los Angeles and New York) and the League of Professional Theatre Women fought to correct that omission. The American Film Institute's Directing Workshop for Women, in which I was lucky enough to be included, gave small grants and visibility to aspiring women directors in the industry, enabling them to make films. When I was hired to direct <u>Another World</u>, a daytime television show on NBC, I was the first female director on a show that had been on the air for 12 years. When I joined the Directors Guild of America I received mail addressed to **Mr**. Lenore DeKoven for the first 6 months of my membership, probably because I had joined as a full director rather than as the customary assistant director or production assistant. Thus, the issue of the pronoun to be used in reference to the director was huge for me. In the dictionary, the second option listed for "he" is "used to represent any person whose sex is not specified." But I was unwilling to settle for that. As you read you will discover my solution—an unwieldy one at best. The use of his/her and he/she is all that I could come up with after much thought.

Many of my former students are now teaching all over the world and the awareness of that fact became one of the reasons for my capitulation. Hence this attempt to record in writing, much as I teach it, the approach I have developed over the years in courses at UCLA, NYU, and Columbia. The many calls and emails I've received from former students with questions about specific elements of my approach to the craft, perhaps now dimly remembered, made me aware of the necessity of some tangible form of reference to preserve the shape and logic of the approach. In addition, former graduate film and theatre students who have run into me at various industry events and greeted me with an accusing "I couldn't get into your class! When are you writing the book?" have also served to nudge me toward this adventure.

The pages that follow are certainly not the whole story, which I suspect might only be accomplished with a human presence or some sort of accompanying visual aid, but represent my best effort to provide a helpful reference and resource to students, professional directors, and teachers of directing.

Acknowledgments

This book would not have been possible without the ongoing encouragement and support of family, friends, and my students, past and present.

In particular I must thank Jason Cirker for his invaluable input and editing assistance and Christine Cirker for her creative cover design ideas and computer wisdom. I am indebted to my dear friend and colleague Annette Insdorf for sharing the tapes of her celebrated <u>Reel Pieces</u> series with me. My thanks go to Liz Woodman and Judy Henderson for allowing me to include their casting expertise. The critical analysis and suggestions from Bill Neff, Sheldon Schiffer, Cecil Esquivel, and Jason Lucero, as well as the loyal and wise assistance of Lally Ross, helped immeasurably and I am truly grateful to each of them.

Above all, my heartfelt thanks goes to Ang Lee for the gift of his beautiful Foreword.

And to all my students here and throughout the world, thank you for all that you have taught me.

Introduction

Some years ago I heard a story that I love to tell my students. It concerns the saintly Mother Theresa whose humane works are legendary. It is said that when she arrived at heaven's gate, God was waiting to greet her.

> *"Welcome, welcome," he cried. "We are overjoyed to see you."*
> *"Thank you, O Lord," murmured Mother Theresa, bowing humbly.*
> *"Dear Mother Theresa," said God. "You have lived such an exemplary life. You have done so much for humanity. You deserve to be richly rewarded. I'd like to give you a gift. What can I grant you? What have you always wanted and never had the opportunity to receive or pursue?" Mother Theresa bowed her head in deep thought. When she looked up at God finally her eyes shone.*
> *"Well," she smiled shyly, "I've always wanted to direct!"*

Everyone wants to be in show business. The media-driven aura of glamour and wealth is irresistible. A recent cab driver, aware that he was driving me to Columbia University, asked me what I taught there. When I told him I was in the Graduate Film Division he immediately wanted to give me a screenplay he had written. Many would love to be actors, but the obvious demands and risks are daunting. But directing! Ahhh, that looks easy. You tell people when to move and where to sit and stand, make sure they say the right words, pick the sets, costumes, and music, and, to top it all off, you're the boss and everyone looks up to you. Or at least that's the common misconception regarding the director's craft. What follows is intended to dispel that misconception and introduce the reader to the true complexity of the task and an approach that offers the means with which to tackle it. Having studied with some of the theatre and film greats of the post-Stanislavski era, I have over the years synthesized—from the infinite variety of their teaching—a functional process and a concise language that I use to simplify that task and to facilitate the all-important collaboration between actor and director in a time-saving and clear manner.

Well, then, what *is* it that we do? What is the nature of this craft we call directing? If we attempt to express it in its simplest and most basic terms, what defines our craft? You will find as we progress that my effort is always to reduce things to their simplest forms or, at times, find the lowest common denominator. That is because our work is often so complex that we need to address it layer by layer. Let me caution you at this point as I do with my classes. Because our craft is a layered process I will present it as such. As you embark on this journey with me I must ask for your patience. The complete understanding of the approach cannot be realized until the end of the trip.

What makes the work so complex? Well, that returns us to the question—what are we doing? What do directors and actors do? I get many answers when I ask this question of a class.

"We're putting together elements to make a film or a play"
"We're telling stories"
"We're making a script come to life"
"We're communicating our ideas to the world," etc.

Yes, all of these answers are true. We are storytellers and communicators. But what is at the foundation of *all* that we do?

We are recreating human behavior. That is basically what we are doing—even when it involves science fiction, animals, animation, etc.—as it all stems from us, from our brains, our behavior, the sum total of what we are as human beings. Well, you say, when someone asks me what I do for a living, I'm not going to say I recreate human behavior. After all, there's a lot more to directing than that. That's true, but remember, we're attempting to break down this very complex pursuit into layers that we can gradually assemble into the whole result. But what are these layers?

One cannot recreate behavior unless one makes a study of it in all its multifaceted and fascinating forms. Indeed, that study is a dynamic and ever-changing lifetime pursuit. It provides the food of the creative artist, the resource and the reservoir from which the memory can retrieve what it needs for the process of recreation.

And the study halls are all around us wherever there is humanity behaving.

As a young girl just graduated from high school and too young to begin college, I attended the Dramatic Workshop of the New School for Social Research where Stella Adler and Herbert Berghof were teaching acting. I had some notable classmates, among them the great Maureen Stapleton and the legendary Marlon Brando. We were all young and eager to experiment and learn and the environment of the Workshop seemed an ideal place to grow. But I remember hearing Brando talk about how the New York subway at rush hour was his real classroom. And Maureen would tell us stories about her bread job at the telephone company. Both of these environments offered a host of opportunities to study human behavior.

The next time you are in a room full of people—a dentist's waiting room, a restaurant, a party, or on public transportation— observe and study. What are people doing? They're all in the same circumstance but is everyone the same? What are the similarities in their behavior? What are the differences? Can you tell what they're thinking? Can you guess what their occupations might be? How do they relate to their environment? What makes some people talk to each other so loudly that they invade the space of those around them? What makes others seem to be attempting to shut out the world around them?

At some point during the first meeting with my class, I will shout to the group "freeze just as you are!" and then ask the startled students to look around without moving their bodies. Although they are all sitting in a classroom listening to me, each one at that moment is doing something different from the others. One leans forward, hands on knees. One chews on a pencil, head tilted upward. Another stretches out in his chair, fingers drumming on his notebook. What is making them behave differently? And how can we believably recreate this scene with all of its variety? Because that is what the director must do. In arriving at movement for either the stage or the camera the director must recreate the life of each and every character present in a given circumstance—must figure out in collaboration with the actors what each might be doing, why they might be doing it, and how they might be doing it. The choices will be based on the knowledge of the script and characters and an understanding of what motivates the behavior that might occur in the scene.

How then do we conduct this study? *It is not enough to say we must observe. What is required of any creative artist is sharpened sensory perception—all five senses: sight, hearing, touch, taste, and smell—must be activated in order to fully realize the work implied by this very general word, observation.* (You will find in Chapter 2 that exercises for the sharpening of sensory perception are part of the basic training of the actor.) Yet alas, our contemporary environment conspires to rob us of the very attributes we need the most, and even more so if we live in an urban area. Take the sense of sight for example. We look, but do we really see? We are hurtling through life at such a pace in the ever-growing quest for creature necessities and comforts and the fulfillment of goals and dreams that we are forced to overlook most of the visual information we receive on a moment-to-moment basis.

An experiment that I often try on a new class always bears this out. It is usually a room containing about 12 people and after about an hour together I ask one individual to turn his or her back on us and tell us what each of us is wearing that day, in as much detail as possible. Invariably the response is something like this:

> *"Well, the woman next to me is wearing blue jeans and a tee shirt, and the guy in the next seat has on striped pants—I think they're a sort of brown. And Mary has on a red blouse and a kind of loose skirt. Oh, and John has on really dirty sneakers." (agonized pause) "That's all I can remember."*

A vague and general response about clothing, which might be just as general about the behavior of those present, would not enable the director to recall the kind of useful information needed to make specific choices in the recreation of that scene.

Try this on yourself after sitting in a roomful of people for a while. How much are you seeing? And how much can you remember? Indeed we have actually trained ourselves to limit our sensory perception so as to avoid complete saturation and ultimate breakdown as there is such a bombardment of stimuli in our modern society. And yet detail and specificity are so important to our work and a functional memory for detail is essential.

Look at what's happened to our sense of smell. There is so much pollution and proliferation of evil-smelling elements in our air that we limit our breathing in an act of self-protection. Thus, what is the first thing we do on a getaway to the country or the shore? "Aaah," we say as we inhale deeply, perhaps for the first time in a while, "smell the air!" City dwellers have trained them-selves to shorten their breathing intake so as not to offend their senses.

The loss of hearing in the current generation has been a topic of growing concern as the decibel levels rise ever higher. Particularly in the urban environment there is so much unwanted noise that we've subconsciously trained ourselves to screen out much of what we hear. In addition, we now have innovations such as the ubiquitous Apple IPod with which to aid us in that screening. Try this: Sit very still, close your eyes, and concentrate on hearing everything you possibly can. You will be surprised by what sounds emerge that you hadn't even noticed before.

Sadly, even our sense of taste has been compromised. Because of mass production and the growing use of chemicals in our food, our taste buds seem to adjust to the tastelessness (as in the wax on our tomatoes) by craving more spices and other exotic additives.

The first order of business in the process of developing both the actor's and the director's crafts is the conscious sharpening of ones' sensory perception. It is a process of reclamation; a return to the child state at which time your senses were still pure and uncompromised.

Watch a small child at play. See how an infant examines an object by touching it, smelling it, tasting it. It doesn't matter where it has been or whether it is caked with dirt. There is no censoring, no inhibition, no repression. These are all learned responses that the adult creative artist must learn how to eliminate. Watch some of our most brilliant actors, i.e., Robert DeNiro or Marlon Brando in his early days. These actors have the ability to communicate an almost child-like, no-holds-barred purity in the way in which they relate to the world around them. Their simplicity and sense of investigation, probing, and discovery make us believe that we are seeing the truth.

The question that follows is that once having made this study of behavior, how do we then communicate our understanding, knowledge, and vision to the actor? How do we create a collabora-tive process that helps the actor make choices for the character? Ah, there's the rub! This is the point at which it all so often breaks down. Because in actuality we have not learned the language of the actor and the actor often finds it necessary to translate our lan-guage into something useful, something he/she is able to do. Often that translation will be incomplete or inaccurate through no fault of the actor. Our early schooling provides us with a prose-oriented awareness of how to communicate. We tend to speak in sentences and paragraphs. We use adjectives and adverbs unsparingly in an effort to paint a word picture of what we want the listener to know. Too often these words are of little use to the actor. It is always a surprise to my students when I inform them that the course they are about to experience actually involves the learning of a new language. We must learn the language of the actor, which, you will find, is quite different from that to which you are accustomed and have used successfully all your lives.

In the chapters that follow we will explore an approach to the craft of directing actors that goes beyond the common misconceptions of the task. I've stated that it is a language course and that the craft involves a layering process. Chapter by chapter we will learn how to build these layers into the structure of complex human behavior that will tell our stories. As we progress we will also be acquiring a new vocabulary—a kind of shorthand of communication that will enable us to share our vision and get what we need with speed, clarity, and specificity, not only with our actors, but with the rest of our creative team as well. As with the learning of any new language or expertise, I ask for your patience and persistence. By the time you reach the end of this book you will have an additional set of tools with which to pursue this most demanding craft.

The Actor and Training

2

It is my firm belief that any director worth his/her salt should have a grounding in the specifics of the actor's training. However, if you are a trained actor or a director who has experienced actor training, you might want to skip the following chapter and go right to Chapter 3.

In both narrative film and theatre the actors provide the means by which we recreate human behavior and tell our stories. How do they arrive at the choices they make to become the characters in the scripts? And what is their language, their vocabulary? If we as directors are to communicate with them successfully, we must have some insight into their process. That word *process* should be plural, actually, as each actor usually has his or her own *modus operandi*, developed as a result of training and/or experience. It is currently assumed that an individual desirous of a career as an actor will seek some kind of training. In the old days, actors were often hired, particularly in film and later in television as well, for their *type* or their *look* with little attention to any ability to act. It was often casting by persona or charisma or blatant sex appeal. Many of the famous stars of yesteryear learned on the job and sometimes sought training in midcareer as demands changed. But as competition increased along with the skill of plastic surgeons who can now make anyone commercially beautiful, actors realized that they needed acting skill and sought training as a means to developing their craft and sharpening the competitive edge.

In most cases, the training now prevalent in this country derived originally from the basic concepts put forth by the famous Russian director Constantine Stanislavski. But like the old telephone game in which the initial word becomes something very different after passing through 20 listeners and repeaters, there are now many different versions and approaches to the training, many stemming from the original root but some altogether different. We will look into some of the approaches to actors' training in the chapter on casting.

EXERCISES

In order to viscerally understand the actors' process I firmly believe that directors should experience some of the basic actors' training exercises. After all, what actors have to do is the same as what we as directors do on a larger, more all-encompassing scale: we have to recreate human behavior. And to do that we have to sharpen our sensory perception and hone our ability to recall experience. A dancer must maintain his body, which is his instrument, by doing daily exercises at the barre. Similarly, I believe that the actor and director must have certain barre exercises with which to keep sensory perception and memory functioning at optimum levels.

RELAXATION EXERCISE

Unlike the exercises you would do in the gym to get washboard abs or tighten the thighs, these demand a specific preparation. You must be completely relaxed. And, while this sounds simple, I've found that it is extremely difficult for an individual to fully relax under most everyday stresses. Yet this is what an actor must do in what is sometimes the most trying of circumstances: in the wings before an entrance on stage or on a noisy, crowded film set. *And yet the ability to relax quickly and effectively is of prime importance, for tension reduces the blood supply to the brain* and not only limits sensory perception, but often impairs memory as well. When an actor repeatedly goes up on his lines (forgets them), I look for the cause. Is it something in the logic of the writing or is it the tension created by other factors, such as the presence of the camera or the live audience? It's most often the tension. In fact, I often suggest that the actor do push-ups or sit-ups so as to ease the tension with physical exertion. Here's the exercise for relaxation we do in class.

Sit in a chair, making yourself as comfortable as possible
Shut out the world (close eyes if necessary) and focus on your body
Let your arms hang, let your stomach hang, let your head hang
Focus on your toes and relax them
Move to your feet and ankles and relax them
Relax your calves, knees, and thighs
Relax your stomach, let it stick out
Relax your diaphragm and breathing
Consciously relax your fingers, then your wrists, then your elbows, and then your arms
Relax your neck and shoulders (this is often the most intense seat of tension)
Relax your jaw, let it hang
Relax your mouth
Relax your eyes and forehead
Breathe

At first this may seem to be slow and laborious, but if you do it regularly you'll find that you can arrive at a relaxed state more quickly as your body learns to respond.

Another exercise that I picked up from a noted dance group choreographer mainly involves breathing but is very effective in helping an individual to relax and center focus.

Inhale fully, mouth closed, to a mental count of one
Exhale to the count of one
Inhale to the count of one, two
Exhale to the count of one, two
Inhale to the count of one, two, three
Exhale to the count of one, two, three,

and so on until you reach the count of ten, inhaling and exhaling. The steady increase of length of breath will slow your pulse rate considerably and help you achieve a much calmer and more focused state.

Once having reached a state of complete relaxation, how does the actor go about recreating the human behavior of a character in all its complex forms? Well, I believe that the process involves using parts of the actor's own physical, emotional, intellectual, and psychic self. The actor must be able to extract relevant elements of ones own being and reassemble them into different combinations to create a whole new mode of behavior suitable to the character in the text. To use the dance parallel once more—dancers, particularly jazz dancers, do what they call *isolation* exercises, i.e., head rolls, shoulder rotations, rib cage side to side moves, hip swivels, etc. Actors must also learn to first identify and then to isolate parts of themselves so they can reassemble them. It is true that analyzing and attempting to dissect how you walk can tend to inhibit motion since you are accustomed to doing it so reflexively. This investigation and reassembly, seemingly painstaking at the outset, can eventually become reflexive. Remember, we are going to try to reduce this complex pursuit into its simplest forms as we continue to examine the elements of the process. And the first step must always be *relaxation* so as to allow the brain to function at top capacity.

CONCENTRATION

The next step in the process is something many people have difficulty achieving, particularly in our fast-paced, hectic, and distracting contemporary climate. *It is absolutely necessary to be able to concentrate fully, shutting out all distraction.* Theatre rehearsals and stage and film sets are perhaps the busiest and most distracting of places. An actor, in order to pursue this most difficult task of recreation, must be able to shut out external intrusions while still being acutely aware of the actors, environment, and moment-to-moment happenings to which he must respond as part of the work. I'm reminded of an incident that happened in the midst of one of my rehearsals. It was a run-through of Act 1 of a play. I told the actors I didn't want to stop for any direction but would take notes and that they should keep going until the end of the act no matter what so we could start to see the shape of the whole play. But after the second scene, my leading man stopped and said "Lenore, I can hear you taking notes. . . . I can hear the pencil scratching on the paper and it's very distracting!" Well of course I had to take notes. The problem was that the actor's insecurity at that stage of rehearsal seemed to sharpen his hearing but messed up his concentration. He was thinking about what he might be doing wrong that caused me to take a note rather than trusting his organic involvement and fully concentrating on the moment. Thus, learning the art of full *concentration* is key to the process.

RECALL

The third important demand in the process is the ability to *recall* experience in detail. *I think of the actor's brain as though it were a very advanced computer*. It stores memory just as a computer does and it responds to stimuli just as though one were pressing a key on the keyboard. Thus we will see as we progress with these exercises how pressing certain keys of the actor's brain by recalling certain sensory details cannot only recreate the experience, but also reproduce the sensation and emotion connected with the experience.

These then are the three requisites: *relaxation, concentration*, and *recall*. They form the starting point of the actor's craft. Most of the actor's barre exercises are designed to work and stretch the muscles that enable us to fully pursue these three steps. Of course it is also necessary to sharpen our powers of *observation* of the details of human behavior. If we do not allow ourselves to fully use our sensory perception in order to observe, we will have little to recall. Here are some samples, but remember, these are exercises for training and preparation. You would never see a dancer stopping in the middle of a ballet to do pliés. Likewise, we should not find an actor doing any of these exercises in the middle of a scene.

There seem to be some common misconceptions about the exercise known as *sense memory*—what it is and what it is used to accomplish. I've heard entry-level actors saying things like "Since I have to cry in this audition I'll do a sense memory when I get to that spot." In my purview, sense memory is one of the exercises designed to enable the actor to develop the muscles that allow him/her to gain access to his/her emotional life and that of the character. It would be folly to stop in the middle of an audition to do an exercise!

SENSE MEMORY EXERCISE

I ask my students to do the following:

Select a very simple task that you perform routinely, choosing something that has a minimum number of steps.
Concentrate on the details of the object used in the performance of the task. Observe it as though you'd never seen it before, noting as many specific details as possible.

Perform the task, observing the sensory detail as you do it. Use as many senses as possible: touch, smell, sight, hearing, taste. Try to see all the marks, dents, scars, colors, etc. on the object. Run your fingers over the object to get the feel of depressions, scales, roughness, smoothness, etc. Does the object have any smell? Does it make any sound when you move it or shake it? Can you taste it? Examine the object as a baby would, without the inhibitions bred by knowledge of the appropriate.

Perform the task again and again, slowing down the normal rate of doing to allow yourself to concentrate.

Then remove the object. Take time to recall the object's details.

Recreate the entire task as though the object were still in hand but without the actual object.

Do not be tempted to simply mime the task or indicate it generally. *The whole purpose of the exercise is to sharpen your ability to observe, recall, and recreate sensory detail.*

Often when we do this exercise in class, students are tempted to "show" the task to their peers who are watching as audience, hoping that this will enable the communication of what the object was and what they were doing with it. But, as I keep pointing out to them, these are *selfish* exercises. They are not designed to enable the actor to communicate with an audience. The aim is not to make sure anyone gets it. The aim is only to strengthen the muscles of observation and recall.

Here are some samples of useful choices for this exercise:

- Putting on your watch: Details of the dial, the watchband, what the dial and band are made of, the sound, if any, the weight of the watch, how it feels on the wrist, etc.
- Combing or brushing your hair: Details of the brush or comb, of the touch of the object on the hair, of the resistance of the hair to the object, details of the hair itself, etc.
- Pouring juice into a glass: Details of the glass, details of the container holding the juice, the liquid, the smell, the temperature of the container, the weight of both objects, etc.
- Sipping coffee or tea: Details of cup, mug or glass, touch on lips, tongue, taste, weight of object, texture and temperature of liquid, etc.
- Putting on your shoes: Details of shoes, color, material, soles, markings, heels, weight of shoe, details of foot,

specifics of closings (laces, buckles, Velcro, shoestrings), touch of shoe on foot, etc.
- Picking up and opening a book: Details of book—printing, colors, covers, weight, content, etc.

Note that these are all simple and familiar tasks involving one or two objects and a limited number of steps. Here are some samples of less useful choices:

- Taking a shower
- Putting on makeup
- Brushing one's teeth
- Playing basketball, etc.

These are much too complex, containing many sensory details and multiple steps, making them too difficult to accomplish in the way that would make the exercise most useful. Choices like those just given almost always lead the individual into the trap of pantomime, which is meant to perform something to an audience without vocal expression and, since not self-oriented, is counterproductive to the fulfillment of the exercise.

Remember, the observation of detail of the object is of primary importance. You would be surprised at how much detail there is in a simple object like a comb. What are the colors? What are the markings? What is printed on it? Are there any teeth missing? What is its length and width? What is it made of? How does it feel to the touch? and so on.

It is also important to remember to slow the process of recall and recreation down to allow yourself the time to pursue the exercise fully. These days our lives are so full that we tend to speed everything up so we can meet the demand to accomplish everything. Speed is counterproductive to the fulfillment of these exercises.

RECALL EXERCISES

An exercise that I find wonderfully stretching and fun to do is the *animal exercise*. This involves observing an animal—domestic or wild (the latter preferably at the local zoo)—in as much detail as possible for as long a period as necessary to enable oneself to recall not only motion (which involves only sense of sight), but also perhaps smell, touch, and hearing. Then try to recall as much detail as possible after leaving the animal's presence. After taking as much time as necessary to remember as much as you can, attempt to recreate the animal with your own body or, in other words, become the animal. This exercise not only develops sensory observation and recall, but also encourages physical awareness and use of the whole body. Of course if you do the exercise in class in front of your teacher and peers, it also helps develop concentration and encourages the abandonment of self-consciousness and inhibition.

Another exercise that is one of my favorites because it leads students into another area of the fine arts is as follows.

Find a painting—oil or watercolor preferably—that you can study for a period of time either in a museum or gallery or in your own or someone else's home. Observe it with as many senses as possible (don't attempt to touch or taste in a gallery or museum or you'll have the guard confronting you!) for as long as it takes to commit every possible detail to memory. The next day, or even the following week, try to recall all the details of that painting. Then describe what you recall to a listener, or the class, in enough detail so that the painting will be recreated in the mind's eye of the listener. A successful recall will often enable the listener to identify at the very least the artist if not the actual painting.

It is important to remember that with these and any other exercises, the first order of business must be to relax fully before attempting the recall. It is only in a completely relaxed state that you will be able to function at optimum capacity. *Also remember that these exercises, unlike those I'm about to describe, are designed to exclude any emotion. Emotion tends to complicate or obscure the ability to recreate.* So if the object or animal or painting selected seems to engender an emotional response so strong that it takes over and impedes the ability to observe and/or recall in specific detail, choose something else.

PHYSICAL STATE OF BEING RECALL

Here is a more complex exercise using the process developed in the previous set that does involve feelings.

Lie down on a bed or the floor.
Relax completely (but don't fall asleep!).

Try to think of a particular occasion when you experienced extreme
heat. Wait until you've actually pinpointed the event before
proceeding slowly, a step at a time.

Try to remember where you were? Outdoors? Indoors? What was
the space?

Where were you in the space? What were you doing? Sitting?
Lying down? Moving?

What were you wearing? Try to remember the details of your clothing (or lack of it).

What was around you? Try to remember the details of the things
around you.

What was below you? What was above you? Sky? Ceiling? Can
you remember the specific details of the objects around you?
Were there other people with you? What were they wearing?

Keep going over the sensory details in your mind. If you are
relaxed and open you will find that the physical sensation of heat
will return to your body as it did on that occasion. This same exercise can be used for any physical state, i.e., cold, nausea, etc.

Why does this happen? Because, as I have stated, it is my
belief that the brain acts like a computer, storing all experience in
its bank. If, in the process of recall, you punch up certain buttons in
your brain's computer memory associated with the sensory details
of the event, the brain will reproduce the physical state.

All of the aforementioned barre exercises for the actor are
muscle stretches for the most useful and important element in an
actor's preparation of the recreation of a character.

EMOTIONAL MEMORY EXERCISE

The ability to organically reproduce an emotional state or prepare
for the creation of the behavior of the character can be developed
with the same type of exercise. Remember one must always start
with relaxation and concentration. This is particularly crucial in
this exercise because the psyche often buries feelings—especially
painful ones—and the brain has to be as receptive as possible to get
past the inhibitions and blocks that might lurk as obstacles.

Try to remember a time when you experienced deep grief.
Do not try to recall the feeling, just remember the specific occasion. It seems we have difficulty recreating feelings intellectually.

Just as with remembering the feelings accompanying sex, which can be the essence of pleasure, one usually recalls the memory of the feeling rather than the feeling itself. Pushing selected buttons of the brain/computer by recalling the sensory detail of a given experience signals the body to actually experience again the accompanying emotion.

When you are sure you have selected a specific time, proceed as in the physical state exercise. Relax, concentrate, and recall:

Where were you when you experienced this grief?
Try to see the place. Were you indoors or outside?
What was above you? Sky? Ceiling? Light fixture? Try to remember it in as much detail as possible.
What was beneath your feet? Floor? Grass? Rug?
Were you sitting down or standing? If sitting, what on?
What objects did you see around you? What were their shapes and colors and textures?
Try to remember the objects in as much detail as possible.
Can you remember what you were wearing? Give yourself time to recall.
Were there any smells in the place?
Were there other people with or around you?
Can you remember what they were wearing?
Were there any sounds? Was anything being said?

Note that the process is more detailed and extensive than that for the physical state. This is because emotions are a tricky business and are often more difficult to access. When we do this exercise in class I usually ask four or five students to work in front of the class and give the remainder the option of doing the exercise in their seats or simply observing. Some students (remember these are directors, not trained actors) will begin to tear up or even sob in a relatively short time—particularly if the recall is a more recent event—but some will have more difficulty getting to the emotion because of a particular block or a lack of concentration and the consciousness of being observed. But on occasion I've asked those students after a time to talk to one another and I am not surprised when, after appearing apparently impassive, the effort to speak causes them to burst into tears.

These exercises stretch certain muscles used in the process of connecting to one's own experiences or emotions for use in recreating aspects of human behavior for the character as it is defined in the text. Many actors find this process useful in preparing to play a scene, particularly when there is a heavy demand for some kind of physical or emotional or psychological *given* at the start.

As an example, let us say the actor must play a sibling who's been told that a brother or sister has died and that the body must be identified. Several elements must be present at the start: grief over the death of a sibling, hope that it might turn out to be somebody else, fear of looking at a dead body, etc. Some or all of these factors lie in what I call the subtext of the character. The subtext is the layer that won't necessarily be found in the actual text, but which is an important part of the full development of the character. Often the created subtext and the behavior derived from it will tell the audience more than the actual dialogue in the text. Some call it the *inner dialogue* or the subconscious. Have you ever been in a situation where you had to smile and nod and agree with a boss (a producer, perhaps) when all you really wanted was to make him go away? That desire to get out of the situation would not be expressed but would affect the smile and nod in a subtle way— because of the desire in the subtext. We will talk much more about the subtext as we progress.

Since the ability to recall and recreate physical, emotional, and psychological experience is key to the craft of the actor, these exercises can be of utmost value. However, I believe that these exercises belong in the province of the scene study class, workshop, or actors' homework. Just as the conductor of a symphony would not stop to teach one of the violinists how to play the instrument, so should the professional director never make the mistake of becoming teacher and introducing these exercises into the rehearsal process. This might be interpreted as an insult, as it would assume that the actor in question didn't have the necessary craft to do the job. At most you might find it necessary on occasion to suggest to the actor that he/she do some sort of *preparation* (perhaps utilizing a recall) to meet the physical or emotional demand of a given scene.

THE METHOD OR A METHOD

Bear in mind that there are many, many ways to develop the craft of the actor. Those that I've described are among the handful that I personally have found to be useful both as an actor and as a teacher of actors and directors. But there are other equally effective methods and approaches and it is up to the individual actor to find his or her own modus operandi. I generally suggest to young actors seeking advice about training that they try several different teachers and approaches and then make a choice in terms of what seems to work best for their individual needs. To me it's like buying a pair of shoes; you must find just the right fit.

As a young girl—having acted by the seat of my pants since the age of 7 and having been heavily influenced by my actor–father who trained at the Theatre Guild and hung out with members of the Group Theatre (perhaps opposite ends of the spectrum)—I sought various teachers who were known at the time to be proponents of the Stanislavski approach. There was much excitement about The Method with a capital M, and some teachers studied or visited the master and then purported to teach his newly evolving approach. In addition to my experience at the New School with Herbert Berghof, after graduating from college I moved on to Lee Strasberg and then, in slow succession, Stella Adler, director Harold Clurman, and another director named David Alexander (where my classmates included Jack Lemmon and Cliff Robertson). Each had something to offer, which fell under the heading of The Method approach, yet although they all had points of similarity and the common goals of organic truth, dramatic reality, and gut-level involvement, each taught something different.

What I did ultimately is what I advise my acting and directing students to do: Experience as many approaches as you can; try them out, give them each your best shot, and then select that which works best for you. It is indeed a one from teacher A and one from teacher B process until you put together your own approach, tailor-made especially for you. So that what is evolved is **your method** rather than The Method (which has long since become such a hybrid as to be almost unidentifiable). My belief is that each artist should have his own method, and after I've shared my approach with you in its totality, I hope you will do just as I've suggested: take what works best for you, discard what doesn't, and perhaps add what you pick up elsewhere. You will, ultimately, have your own modus operandi, your own method.

A piano is an 88 key instrument. The keys on different pianos all look the same, but each has a different touch, tone, heavy or light action, unique sound. *The challenge for the director then in this process of communication with the actor is learning the actor's instrument.* How is the instrument trained? How does this actor ply his craft? How can you best help the actor to arrive at the behavior of the character you want to see? Stated another way, how can you best gain access to the keys of the actor's computer/brain?

There are so many individuals teaching acting currently. Some are descendants of the original proponents of The Method. Some have revised and reshaped approaches so that they are barely recognizable and have become simply a method, but pretty much all come from the same root and although the vocabulary and/or terminology may be somewhat different, most actors, regardless of training, seem to be able to comprehend and translate for themselves a direction from a director who is method oriented as well as from the director who knows little or nothing about the actors' craft. The process of translation in the latter case is much more extensive, however, and leaves much room for misunderstanding and wasted time in communication.

Every actor is different—a different instrument that must be regarded individually in addition to or sometimes despite what it says on the actor's résumé about the training. I'm reminded of an actor I admired tremendously named Kim Stanley who emerged in the fifties as a great talent about the same time as Marlon Brando and others of his ilk. As a young actress I'd been so impressed with and envious of the accessibility of Kim's emotional life. When I saw her in an off-Broadway play in which every night she had to weep bitterly I was compelled to find out how she managed it. One night I ran into her at an actors' hangout and put the question to her. "Oh," she said with a twinkle in her eye, "What I do is dig my fingernails into the skin on my wrist so hard that it hurts like hell. That makes the tears come and I just build it from there." I never found out if she was pulling my leg or being honest. But I wouldn't be a bit surprised if it was the latter. Whatever works! If you can locate it, I urge you to see the film <u>The Goddess</u> (1958) starring Kim Stanley with screenplay by Paddy Chayefsky.

We will go into more specifics about this variety of technique and its effect on the actor–director relationship when we get to the casting phase of the work. The important point is that I believe that the more the director can make himself aware of the possibilities vis á vis the actor's process and perhaps even experience some of the craft training viscerally, the easier it will be to connect to each actor's instrument.

In fact, many of the directors I most admire started their careers as actors: Sidney Lumet began acting on the stage at the tender age of 9 in an epic play called <u>The Eternal Road</u>, directed by Max Reinhardt. Sidney Pollock is still appearing as an actor, sometimes in films he's directing (see <u>Tootsie</u> with Dustin Hoffman). Elia Kazan was an actor member of the renowned Group Theatre. Robert Redford won an Academy Award for his shrewdly chosen first directorial effort. <u>Ordinary People</u>, a small canvas, actor-driven film, is a perfect example of how a truly constructive actor–director relationship can produce a most successful result. Many of our contemporary stars, secure in their knowledge of the acting craft and aware that good acting is so important to the success of a project that it can even make up for other deficiencies, have taken on directorial assignments. Clint Eastwood, perhaps the most prolific, Paul Newman, Benjamin Bratt, Selma Hayek, Jodie Foster, Denzel Washington, Edward Norton, and Liv Ullman are among the most notable on a long list.

Many of my directing students, who initially rebel against having to do actor exercises and act in scenes with each other as part of the Columbia University Graduate Film program, find it so insightful that they eventually consult with me on what acting classes they might take during the summer break. If you are a director who has had no actor training or are planning to become a director, I strongly urge you to join a beginning or intermediate acting class as part of your research and investigation of the craft. If you do not have time to participate in a scene class, which requires outside rehearsal with an acting partner, at the very least find a class that will allow you to sit in and observe.

The Actors' Vocabulary

3

As children we learn to speak and read, and as we grow we develop a language with which to communicate with one another and share our ideas and thoughts verbally and in various forms of writing. By the time we reach adulthood we are secure in the knowledge that we are masters of a functional language. However, I am about to undermine that security.

You see, the language we've learned is based on a prose structure derived from books and filled with sentences, paragraphs, adjectives, adverbs, and a whole slew of descriptive verbiage, which is of little value to the needs of the actor. While it has served us so well in most circumstances, it often, unfortunately, results in clutter and confusion in the brain of the actor and therefore is actually counterproductive. Students in my directing actors classes register bewilderment when I declare at the start that the course is about embarking on the discovery of a new language. We as directors must collaborate with actors on their terms and in their language—or with their vocabulary. And therefore we must agree to lay aside what we think we know and the way we've been expressing ourselves easily for years. We must attempt to replace that with a whole new set of words and a whole new perspective. It's a bit startling to say the least, rather like being told suddenly that you have to change your walk when you've been perambulating successfully all your life.

When asked what they want to hear from a director, many actors on interview and talk shows say "little or nothing" or "less talk." Because too often the director, reflecting his/her own uncertainty as to whether it's getting through, will go on and on repeating or rephrasing the thought in the hope that it's being made clear. All the director is really doing is jamming up the actor's instincts,

21

reflexes, and processes to the point of utter confusion and sometimes even total inhibition. Just recently on <u>Inside the Actors Studio</u>, the TV series on Bravo, I heard Sarah Jessica Parker echo what I've heard from actors through the years. "I have to put my hands over my ears and curl up into my lap," she said so as not to be bombarded with too much of the kind of information that is so destructive to the process.

During my period of study with Lee Strasberg, I was often both delighted and impressed when he made a cogent point about directing. But then he would continue to talk on and on about the point, repeating and elaborating on its meaning until I lost the thread of the original thought entirely. I learned to take notes immediately after the first few sentences of his brilliant wisdom and then shut the rest out.

Since it is my belief that the brain functions like a computer—in the sense that if you push certain buttons you will evoke organic responses hidden somewhere in the memory—and since the "push" in the case of the director must come from the use of words that must communicate the visions or pictures in the head of the director, it seemed necessary to create a vocabulary that would accomplish this as quickly and efficiently as possible. Thus I call it a kind of shorthand communication with which to trigger responses from the actor without burdening him/her with the unnecessary trimmings of prose sentences and paragraphs. *Simple words and phrases, universally understood, are needed for the direct and immediate transfer of the director's suggestions.*

As human behavior is so complex, the challenge of distilling all the intricate layers of the infinite variety of possibility is daunting. Therefore, I have attempted to find a vocabulary that will not only isolate those layers, but also reduce the language describing them to its simplest, most accessible state. The challenge is to choose those words that might have the most universal or, in other words, the most expected effect. However, because human beings are so complex, there will always be surprises and we must be prepared for them.

At this point I usually remind my students that in this craft, as indeed in all the arts, nothing is ever written in stone. Flexibility must always be the watchword. The only rule is that there are no rules and whatever works is useful. But what we must try to do is make the effort to communicate clearly and specifically so as to minimize misinterpreted translation on the part of the actor. In our work, time is our enemy (and in film particularly, time is money!) and misunderstanding costs time.

To reduce the layers of human behavior to their simplest possible forms in order to construct some kind of outline in the process of discovering and creating the behavior of a given character, I have formulated the following premise based on the awareness that although each person is different there are certain universal similarities:

LIFE NEEDS AND SCENE NEEDS

Each and every human being is motivated by a few handfuls of basic needs that seem to dictate behavior in both the immediate and the overall span of his/her existence. By behavior I mean how the person functions on a moment-to-moment basis, how the person thinks, moves, talks, acts, what choices the person makes, how the person reacts to circumstances and events, relates to other individuals, etc. That which I call needs is sometimes referred to by acting teachers and in books as wants, goals, objectives, the spine, etc. We can break down these very basic needs so that they can be expressed with words that might be able to trigger organic responses in the brain of the actor. It has long been my belief, which recent scientific research now supports, that the brain functions much like a computer so that, in effect, when we communicate we are pressing certain buttons in the brain's computer. For example, I think we can all accept the fact that the need **to get love** is a basic, universal one to which everyone can relate. These are words to which everyone can respond. Here are some of the others that I have found to work well in the process of helping the actor identify the underlying drive or motivating force for the character:

- To prove one's worth
- To get self-worth
- To get security
- To prove oneself superior
- To find one's identity
- To free oneself
- To survive
- To save oneself
- To get self-respect
- To get rid of guilt
- To prove oneself as a man or woman
- To prove one's manhood or womanhood

- To get love
- To destroy oneself or others
- To hold onto someone
- To overcome inadequacy
- To overcome insecurity

This seems to be a short list, but when it is modified by certain words, which again may evoke varied responses from the computer buttons/brain of the actor, the possibilities become much broader:

- To find one's worth
- To hold onto one's worth
- To save one's worth
- To prove one's worth as a man or woman
- To hold onto self-worth
- To find security
- To hold onto security
- To save security
- To prove oneself the superior male or female
- To hold onto superiority
- To save superiority
- To hold onto one's identity
- To save one's identity
- To hold onto self-respect
- To save one's self-respect
- To free oneself from guilt
- To hold onto one's manhood or womanhood
- To save one's manhood or womanhood
- To find love
- To hold onto love
- To save love
- To destroy the pain
- To hold onto the status quo

This second group sometimes involves changing just one word. Yet that small adjustment might make a startling change in the behavior of the character that the actor is attempting to create. The word *find* punches up a different set of buttons in the actor's brain than the word *prove* and when you utter the word *save* you might well get an organic urgency in the actor's response that you failed to get by saying "do more" or "make it more intense."

In a case where it becomes necessary to hire an actor who is somewhat older than the age of the character called for in the script, I've found that often the use of the word *find* in the life need (as in *find one's worth*) helps the actor arrive at the desired youth. This is logical as the younger one is, the more likely that everything is a search or a discovery. Conversely, a younger actor playing a role that is older than his own age might use the word *regain* (as in *regain one's worth*) in the life need to give him more maturity, since a more experienced individual might well have endured the loss of worth at some point in his/her life.

It is true that these are very basic needs that we all have most or all of the time. So what value does this awareness have for the actor and director creating a character? Ah, there's the trick. This is where selection or choice comes in. *For though we all have all these needs some or all of the time, it is what we place in priority that makes each of us different from the other.* The individual whose priority need is **to get love** will respond very differently to a set of circumstances than an individual whose priority need is **to prove his/her worth**.

For example:

(She sits at table. He enters with flowers.)
HE: So sorry. Have you been waiting long?
SHE: You might have called me. You're late.
HE: I stopped to get these. (Hands her flowers.)
SHE: And that took you an hour?

If SHE's priority need is **to get love**, she might chide HE for being late and laugh at his excuse

If SHE's priority need is **to prove worth**, she might accuse HE on her first line and reject his excuse by walking away, leaving him holding the flowers.

THE WHO AM I EXERCISE

Often in classes I will ask for a volunteer without providing information as to what I will ask of the student. A brave soul will amble toward the front of the class awaiting instruction from me.

"Okay John," I say, "Tell us all about yourself."
Usually there is stunned silence at first. Then perhaps a question:

"Can I sit down or must I stand?" says the student.
"Please stand," I answer.

The student will then begin a sometimes rambling, sometimes humorous, sometimes awkward response that might last for as little as 2 or as many as 10 minutes.
For example:

> *"Well I went to Yale and majored in Economics because that's what my parents wanted me to do. But then I heard that if you joined the Drama Club you could meet girls." (The class laughs.) "So I did and then I got completely hooked on theatre and decided to change my major. My brother, who is older than me, was working for a film company and during the summer he got me a job on a shoot and that was the beginning of a whole new world for me." Often the student will stop and ask, "Is that enough?" "No, keep going," I answer. Perhaps the student shifts position at this point or reacts with impatience or a shrug. "Umm, I've always thought of myself as an outgoing person, but this is very hard for some reason. . . ." (A long pause.) "My family is very concerned about my future. My dad is an accountant and it's hard for him to accept my choices, especially since it's clear that my brother isn't going to take over the business some day . . ." etc.*

"Okay" I say when the student falls silent finally. "That's enough. Thank you." As the individual returns to his seat muttering "I'll never volunteer again," I challenge the class. "This was not John. This was a character in a play or screenplay. You got a fairly limited text, but you were able to observe the behavior of the character. What did you learn that would guide your choices if you were asked to recreate this character?" And, of course, the first responses are usually in terms of what the students heard John say.

"Well, he's educated and he must be smart because he got into Yale," says one.
"We know he's more into art than commerce," cracks another.
"He seems to have issues with his brother. He mentioned him a couple of times" says a third.

So I call their attention to clues other than the words themselves and point out that John may have been making the whole thing up, improvising to satisfy my demand. How do we know if what he says is the truth or simply a scenario? And I urge them to recall his movement, his body language. Who did he look at most of the time and when did he change his gaze? When did he seem comfortable and when at odds with what he was telling us? I remind them that he did volunteer, which is a clue to the character, that he did obey me when I insisted he continue. How did he present himself? Was he soft-spoken? Timid? Aggressive? Confrontational? What did he *do*? This is most often more revealing than what a person says. How would we analyze this character and in this analysis identify the *subtext* of the character? How would we make a choice of priority need for this character?

Let us start with the fact that John volunteered, almost in spite of himself. What made him do that? Well, he must have had some need in the immediate sense that motivated him to get up. What did he want from us? This leads us to the discovery that there are not one but two priority needs motivating an individual's behavior: the overall or **life need**, which spans the entire life of the individual and/or character in the script, and the immediate or **scene need**, which is the motivating force of the present situation. What is really essential to understand in this process of analysis of behavior is the relationship between these two needs. What one wants in the immediate sense, or scene, is **in order to** get what one wants in the overall or life of the individual. And so in the work of analyzing and making choices of needs for the recreation of a character, all of the clues given in the text of the play or screenplay, all of the knowledge gained in the study of human behavior, and all of our own intuition as human beings must come into play.

In the exercise just given, which I call the WHO AM I exercise, we not only have the spoken text, but the actual behavior of the character to help us make the choices.

SCENE NEEDS

What are these Scene Needs in our simplified working vocabulary? Well, they are pretty much identical to those listed previously with all of the possible variations: to prove one's worth, to find one's worth, to save one's worth, etc. However, there are a few others that really serve only for the immediate circumstance or scene and would be very questionable as useful for the entire life of a character, i.e.,

- To get approval
- To seduce someone (or everyone)

- To win someone over or as an ally
- To get rid of someone

Going through life with the need to get approval as the motivating force would more likely turn into either the need to prove one's worth or the need to get love. Going through life with the priority need to seduce everyone might be appropriate for a character in the play <u>Marat Sade</u> (which takes place in an asylum) or some similar lunatic demand but would be difficult to pursue!

Remember, we are attempting to develop a kind of shorthand communication. Often a student will ask something like "Well, what about 'getting someone to like you.' Isn't that a possible scene need?" Yes, I will reply. That's a need. But don't you think those words might punch up similar responses in the actor's brain to the words *get approval?* I just happen to think that shorter is better. Remember this is only a small slice of the layers of behavior with which actors must work. For their sakes, shorter is better.

Another favorite question that inevitably surfaces in my classes is "Well, what about taking control?" Control seems to be a major concern for my students and "he wants to take control" is a frequent reply when I ask about the choice of scene need in a rehearsal. It is then necessary to explain that control is achieved by pursuing a combination of needs and actions depending on the text. The audience will then perceive control as the result. But control is not actable until it is broken down into components for the actor. How does one take control? Well, perhaps by manipulation or bending a person to one's will. Component action choices might be to charm, to seduce, to cajole, to warn, to threaten, etc. And why is there the need to take control? Is the need to prove oneself superior or is it the need to hold on to one's security? Too often the director, lacking the actors' vocabulary, will give the actor the result he/she wants the audience to perceive, leaving it up to the actor to figure out the components and how to arrive at that result. The work can ultimately be accomplished that way, but it is more hit and miss and may force the director to take much longer to get what he/she has in mind.

Now we have the potential for constructing what I call **the outline** for the character: **the life need and scene need**. The important thing to remember with this vocabulary is the phrase **in order to**, which is the connective tissue linking the two needs. For example, you wouldn't select a character's scene need as to save himself if his life need is to destroy himself. That would become *to save himself in order to destroy himself*. How do you explain the logic of that? You wouldn't want to ask an actor to pursue the scene need to *destroy himself* with a life need *to get love*. Destroying oneself in order to get love would be an extremely sick if not unplayable outline. Here are some examples of what I call doable outlines.

- to prove one's worth in order to get love
- to get love in order to prove one's worth
- to overcome insecurity in order to prove oneself as a man
- to find one's identity in order to get security
- to seduce in order to prove oneself as a woman
- to free oneself in order to save oneself
- to get rid of guilt in order to free oneself
- to find love in order to find worth as a man
- to get rid of someone in order to prove oneself superior, etc.

You might put a character in continuing deep conflict by choosing

- to free oneself in order to hold onto security
- to get rid of someone in order to hold onto love, etc.

You can see that there are many possible combinations, with **the life need always remaining the same and influencing the behavior of the character for the entire length of the script from beginning to end. The scene need, which must be pursuable for the entire scene from beginning to end, changes scene by scene** to accommodate the characters involved and the demands of each scene on the journey of the script. Choosing the outline allows the actor to connect to and reassemble specific parts of himself, thus enabling the actor to become a character with priorities that motivate behavior other than his own instinctive responses.

CHOOSING THE OUTLINE

Let us go back to our volunteer John, who hopefully by now has recovered from the trauma of acute embarrassment and possible exposure in the process of offering us a character to analyze. What might we choose as a life need for the John character? Remember, we are looking for a set of words that will lie in the subtext, or psyche of the character (as well as in that of the actor recreating the character), and also remember that we are making these choices *for* the character. Just as we don't know a lot about our own subtexts and often go to a therapist to gain insight, so the character usually doesn't know anything about his underlying motivation.

Have you ever gone to an interview for a job or an audition and totally messed it up even though your intelligence told you that you needed to do well? Perhaps it was that sneaky little subtext that dictated your behavior and was telling you *to free yourself* rather than *get security.*

We all have these needs all the time. It's the ones we place in priority that determine our behavior.

Perhaps at this point you might want to return to page 26 and review the substance of John's text. What did he mainly select to talk about? How much did you really learn about him? Did he refer to any romantic relationships? Sexual liaisons? Triumphs? Failures? Did he take us all in or choose to look at only one of us? Was he outgoing or internalized? Aggressive or withdrawn? Although we don't know if he was making it up, note that he chose to talk mainly about family in relation to his life— what his father did and wanted and how his brother influenced the events in his life. Note also that he left out his mother. Then there were allusions to theatre and film and how he seemed to stumble into these areas of interest. Note too that although he volunteered to do heaven knows what, which was a brave act, once he was confronted with the reality he was dying to get out of it. Is he in some kind of conflict? Actually in the case of John, there was so little information that we'd be forced to make some guesses and perhaps provide a bit more background from our own intuition or imagination. Perhaps we can gain more insight by identifying specifically what he *did* from moment to moment.

ACTIONS

This brings us to the next step in our choice-making process of recreating the character. What are the moment-to-moment *doings* that will get us what we want in the scene that will bring us closer to achieving what we want in life? These *doings* which

I call **actions**, are for me the gold of the vocabulary. They enable us to specifically communicate to an actor exactly what his instincts are telling him to do in the pursuit of the needs or what we as directors would like to see him do at any given moment. Thus, we now have a more complete picture of the possibility of choices for the recreation of the character: **What we do on a moment-to-moment basis is in order to get what we want in the scene, which is in order to get what we want in the life of the character**.

To return to the class example, let us say that I ask the class to identify these doings or actions in the John character.

"Well, he seemed to be uncomfortable," responds a student.

"Yes," I reply, "but that is not an action. That is a result perceived by the viewer. We don't want to talk to actors in terms of results if we can avoid it. It is more constructive to think in terms of the ingredients that might produce the desired result. An action should always be expressed as a verb. What did he do that made you aware of his discomfort?"

"He moved around and moved his body"

"Well I would call moving around and general moving of the body more of an activity than an action in the actor's terms we are learning about. In searching for one action verb that might produce this response in the actor, I would choose **to fidget.***"*

"He was trying to be funny" says another student.

"At what point?" I ask.

"When he talked about meeting girls as the reason he got into the theatre stuff."

"Yes, but what was he doing?" I reply.

First, I never use *to be* with actors. *To be funny* is a passive statement. To be—*is* already. The actor is asking "what do you want me to do" not "what do you want me to be?" So how would we recreate that moment when John seemed to be trying to be funny? I would express it as *amuse us*. That is another actor's action verb: **to amuse**.

Now let us find more action verbs that might lead us to the John character's scene and life needs. Together we attempt to identify the moment-to-moment actions: First, he volunteered.

Yes, to volunteer is a verb but is it an actor's verb? Is it doable without dialogue? For that is the true test of a useful actor's verb. Remember that all these action verbs are in the subtext and go under the lines of dialogue in the text just as the needs do. If the actor's brain isn't able to instantly respond to a verb and can't pursue it without any kind of speech, it isn't going to be a useful choice. I might identify the volunteering as the result of the action **to challenge** himself.

Let's see what other actions we might identify:

*"Well I was born in North Carolina and went to grade school and high school there and then I went to Yale and majored in Economics because that's what my parents wanted me to do." (Perhaps the action here was **to impress**.) "But then I heard that if you joined the Drama Club you could meet girls." (The class laughs. Clearly the action is **to amuse**.) "So I did and then I got completely hooked on theatre and decided to change my major (**to discover**). My brother, who is older than me, was working for a film company and during the summer he got me a job on a shoot and that was the beginning of a whole new world for me"(**to boast**?).*

Often the student will stop and ask: "Is that enough?" (**to withdraw** or **to question**). "No, keep going," I answer. Perhaps the student shifts position at this point or reacts with impatience or a shrug (**to fidget, to toss off**). "Umm, I've always thought of myself as an outgoing person, but this is very hard for some reason . . ." (perhaps **to plead** with me to let him off the hook). A long pause (**to ponder**). "My family is very concerned about my future. My Dad is an accountant and it's hard for him to accept my choices, especially since it's clear that my brother isn't going to take over the business some day (**to confide**)" etc.

Now let us examine the possible choices—to challenge, to impress, to amuse, to discover, to boast, to withdraw, to question, to fidget, to toss off, to plead, and to confide—and what do we learn? Perhaps there is conflict in the character, as we seem to have both inwardly directed (withdraw, question) and more assertive, outwardly directed (challenge, amuse, boast, etc.) verbs. The student did volunteer but was obviously nervous and fidgety about doing so. The fact that he wants to be a director, which led him to film school, and wanted to impress the class and me, which caused him to stay with the exercise, might help in making the outline choices. Following this completely hypothetical line of thought, we might perhaps choose for the recreation of the John character the following outline:

To overcome insecurity (scene need) in order to prove his worth (life need).

And the action choices would follow as:

challenge himself in order to overcome insecurity in order to prove his worth,

impress us in order to overcome insecurity in order to prove his worth,

amuse us in order to overcome insecurity in order to prove his worth, and so on.

However, if we wanted to make the John character softer, more vulnerable and eager to please, and yet still place him in a bit of conflict, we might place more importance on his apparent connection to his family and his concern about his father's opinion. We might make a different choice of outline, for example:

To find self worth in order to get love.

Of course, this Who Am I was made up by me simply for purposes of illustration and so we are obliged to refer to the words for clues as to possible choices without being able to observe the individual. In actual work we have every detail of the entire screenplay or script to refer to along with our instincts and intuition and those of the actors with whom we are collaborating helping us make the outline choices.

The important discovery here is that whatever is chosen for the subtext can completely influence the way in which the dialogue is perceived as well as the total behavior of the character. The realization that words of a script can be so changed in meaning by the choices of the actor and director strikes terror in the hearts of the writers in my classes. But indeed, that is the power that directors and actors have over the script and its interpretation. It is the power of choice.

Here's an example of how an action choice lying in the subtext can influence not only the reading of the line of dialogue, but also the behavior and/or activity of the character. Let us take the line "I think I'm going to leave now." The obvious choice might be for the character to walk out of the room, since that is what the words seem to demand.

But what if the actor were to use the action **to escape**? This would increase the speed of the exit greatly as the word escape usually produces a sense of emergency in the actor's computer bank/brain. If I suggested to an actor that he needed to escape, he'd most likely be out the door.

However, what if we chose the action **to threaten** with the words "I think I'm going to leave now?" This would produce a very different result. First, there would be the implied menace, which the word threaten usually evokes in the actor's brain. When we threaten we might not act immediately. So perhaps the character doesn't move as he says the line, but waits to see the response to the threat. This might prove to be a much more interesting choice. Everyone waits to see what is going to happen next. In the more obvious choice of simply walking out, we get a flat, linear acting out of the words, a simple underlining of their obvious meaning. But this is not life, for in life everything we say is affected by what we want, what we are doing to get it, and what that pursuit, along with accompanying obstacles and triumphs, is making us feel.

To repeat, everyone has all the basic needs all the time and it is what each individual puts in priority that makes each of us different from the other. By the same token, the way in which we pursue those needs on a moment-to-moment basis further defines us as individuals.

So the choice of the actions that pursue the needs of a given character will lift that character off the printed page and help the actor create a clearly defined human being, derived from parts of the actor's self, but parts reconstituted and repositioned so as to become a character other than that actor.

HELLO HOW ARE YOU EXERCISE

Often an exercise, which I call **Hello How Are You** will help clarify this concept of actions and needs creating subtext for the dialogue. Two people are assigned the dialogue in the following fragment

Actor 1:   "Hello, how are you?"
Actor 2:   "I'm fine. How are you?"
Actor 1:   "Not so hot."

We give Actor 1 the action **to welcome** and Actor 2 the action **to reject**. At the same time we caution them to pursue the actions and let the words simply come along. We also remind them to start pursuing the action (not necessarily the words) immediately, without waiting for the other actor to begin. We tell Actor 1 to start the dialogue. Now he/she has no difficulty with welcoming on "hello how are you" because those are welcoming words. But the words "not so hot," which seem to dictate sadness or a shrug, will come out very differently with the action to welcome. Actor 2, instead of responding as in ordinary conversation, might actually choose to walk away from Actor 1, as his/her action is to reject. Now the natural response is to react to the received impulse, which would of course change the action. If you are rejected, you might not continue to welcome. But for the purposes of this exercise and this exercise only, it is important to hold onto the action, no matter what, in order to clearly understand how the isolated action choice can affect both spoken word and behavior.

The next step is to switch the action choices while the actors keep the same dialogue, so it will go something like this:

Actor 1: "Hello, how are you?" (The action is now **reject** so he/she might be walking away from Actor 2 or, at the very least, turning his/her back to the other actor.)

Actor 2: "I'm fine. How are you?" (The action is **welcome** so he/she might move toward the other, arms outstretched perhaps.)

Actor 1: "Not so hot." (Still rejecting; he/she has shut Actor 1 out entirely as Actor 2 continues to welcome.)

Next we might switch the dialogue, giving Actor 2 the line "Hello, how are you" and Actor 1 the line "I'm fine, how are you," but keeping the actions as before, i.e., Actor 2 has **to welcome** and Actor 1 has **to reject**. This will illustrate how each actor reacts to and interprets the action word used previously by the other actor. Remember, if you think of the actor as an instrument you must allow for the fact that each instrument, although in the same category, may respond somewhat differently, which is why we try to use the most universally understood vocabulary.

Next we assign a scene need to each actor to add to the action choice. You will note that for this particular exercise only, we are going backward. Ordinarily we would have to start with the life need and then choose the scene need that is pursued in order to pursue the life need. But this is an exercise merely to demonstrate the effects of the outline on the subtext and to isolate parts of behavior. In actual work, an individual would never hang onto an action no matter what. The action would change in response to what the other actor or actors were doing.

Here is an example of possible choices.

Actor 1: action, **to welcome**. Scene need, **to win other actor** with "Hello, how are you?"

Actor 2: action, **to reject**. Scene need, **to free oneself** with "I'm fine, how are you?"

Actor 1: **to welcome** in order **to win** actor 2 "Not so hot."

Here, with the need to welcome in order to win Actor 2, the hello line might have more urgency—be more outgoing. Likewise, the need of Actor 2 to reject in order to free himself might make him/her more intensely anxious to get away.

Again, dialogue may be switched with the actors keeping the same actions and needs.

Actor 2: action **to reject**. Scene need, **to free oneself** with "Hello, how are you?"

Actor 1: action **to welcome**. Scene need, **to win other actor** with "I'm fine, how are you?"

Actor 2: action **to reject**. Scene need, **to free oneself** with "Not so hot."

Alternatively, actions and needs can be switched with actors keeping the same dialogue.

Actor 1: action **to reject**. Scene need, **to free oneself** with "Hello, how are you?"

Actor 2: action **to welcome**. Scene need, **to win other actor** with "I'm fine, how are you?"

Actor 1: action **to reject**. Scene need, **to free oneself** with "Not so hot."

In this last switch the group can observe the difference in how each actor might respond to the same action words. In any case, each combination will produce a different scene as perceived by the class or audience.

It becomes increasingly clear that an audience receives and processes what it sees much more immediately and specifically than what it hears. We pick up visual cues much faster than auditory ones, and the influence of the subtext can completely determine the meaning of the text. This gives the director and actors tremendous power over the written word, a responsibility that can result in either the communication or the destruction of the writer's intent. We will address this aspect of the work in subsequent chapters.

The final phase of the exercise is the adding of the life need. For example, let us choose for Actor 1 the life need **to prove one's worth** so that in putting the whole set together he/she is now welcoming in order to win Actor 2 in order to prove his/her worth. Let us give Actor 2 the life need **to get love** so that his/her outline is to reject in order to free him/herself in order to get love.

Ah, you say. But that life need, to get love, seems to be in opposition to the action and scene need. Precisely so—Have you never experienced a situation where, although you wanted love, you were trying to get it from what you knew might be a potentially destructive candidate? We have put this character into a palpable conflict that will certainly color the way in which Actor 2 pursues to reject in order to free him/herself. It will, in fact, modify the intensity of the pursuit and possibly even make him/her more vulnerable and less likely to keep moving away from Actor 1.

This set of action, scene need, and life need forms the *outline* for the character. Students will sometimes ask if the life need or scene need can change in the middle of the script or scene or if there can be more than one need used. **In my approach there can be only one life need, which must serve the actor from the very beginning to the very end of the script, and one scene need, which must serve for the entire scene from its beginning to its end.**

We can experiment endlessly with different combinations of actions, scene needs, and life needs while keeping the same simple dialogue. There is no end to possible choices and it is amazing to see how this simple change of direction with a few specifically chosen words can create a whole new scene in an instant. Here are some examples of possible choices.

Actor 1: Hello, how are you?—to tease (action) in order to get approval (scene need) in order to get love (life need)
Actor 2: I'm fine. How are you?—to accuse (action) in order to get rid of guilt (scene need) in order to prove one's worth (life need)
Actor 1: Not so hot—to tease in order to get approval in order to get love

This might be the beginning of a lover's quarrel.

Or

Actor 1: Hello, how are you?—to challenge (action) in order to prove his/her worth (scene need) in order to free him/herself (life need)

Actor 2: I'm fine. How are you?—to threaten (action) in order to get rid of him/her (scene need) in order to destroy him/her (life need)

Actor 1: Not so hot—to challenge in order to prove his/her worth in order to free him/herself

This is obviously the beginning of a fight.

Or

Actor 1: Hello, how are you?—to teach (action) in order to prove oneself superior (scene need) in order to prove one's worth (life need)

Actor 2: I'm fine. How are you?—to question (action) in order to get approval (scene need) in order to get love (life need)

Actor 1: Not so hot—to teach in order to prove oneself superior in order to prove one's worth

Here we have the potential for a classroom scene between teacher and young student.

Remember, the dialogue has not changed at all, but the audience's perception of what is taking place is entirely dependent on the subtext informing these words. The fun of this exercise lies in watching how the actors react to the words we are giving them, seeing how the computer buttons in their heads work in response to the word stimuli and how they influence both their bodies physically and their being emotionally.

It is usually at this point that directors and actors begin to beg me for lists. Just as there is a list of possible universal needs for our vocabulary, so might there be one for those wonderfully useful actor's action verbs. For years I have resisted their pleas, mainly because I have always felt that the best way to develop this language is to make discoveries on one's own and then formulate one's own resulting list. Also keep in mind that we are communicating to the individual actor's computer/brain and must take into consideration the fact that some words work all the time, some words work some of the time, and some might work for one actor and not for another. Since responses from the actor appear to be entirely based on stored up memory in that brain and each actor's memory of experience is likely to be different, there are always a few surprises in store for the director. But with the flexibility of an extensive vocabulary, adjustments can be made quickly and easily to arrive at the desired result.

You will notice that I always attach the word *to* in order to remind us that these words are *doings* not *being* and that in this context *the word action does not mean physical response*. Remember that it always lies in the psychological subtext of the character.

ACTION VERB LIST

Here are some of the action verbs I have found most useful. In other books on acting and directing you will perhaps see similar lists of action verbs. But those lists invariably include words that, although identified correctly as verbs, are not what I consider to be useful for the actor's process of creating a subtext. Many of them are results of pursuing several actions. *The question as to whether an action verb is doable has to be measured by the ability of the actor to pursue the action readily without any dialogue* (as it lies underneath the already written text). Does it immediately enable the actor to respond? Bear in mind that every time I work with actors I discover new possibilities and the list grows:

to accuse	to bestow	to comfort
to admire	to boast	to command
to admonish	to brag	to confess
to adore	to brood	to confide
to amuse	to brush off	to confront
to annoy	to buddy up	to congratulate
to apologize	to caress	to cuddle
to applaud	to celebrate	to defend
to attack	to challenge	to deify
to bask	to charm	to demand
to beg	to check out	to destroy
to belittle	to coax	to dis

to discard	to lure	to seduce
to discover	to mock	to seethe
to dismiss	to mother	to shock
to distract	to mourn	to show off
to embrace	to ogle	to sneak
to entertain	to patronize	to soothe
to entice	to perform	to stalk
to erupt	to pester	to startle
to escape	to plead	to strut
to examine	to ponder	to surrender
to explode	to pounce	to tantalize
to exult	to preen	to taunt
to flatter	to prepare	to teach
to flaunt	to primp	to tease
to flee	to probe	to tempt
to flirt	to protect	to test
to gloat	to provoke	to threaten
to grieve	to put down	to toss off
to hide	to question	to triumph
to idolize	to reject	to ward off
to ignore	to rescue	to warn
to impress	to retreat	to welcome
to incite	to ridicule	to withdraw
to inspect	to savor	to worship
to instruct	to scold	to yearn
to invade	to scrutinize	
to invite	to search	

This is of course a partial list to which additions can be made constantly. But it is important to bear in mind that acid test: *does it immediately make one think of something that one can pursue without speaking?* Here are some examples of verbs that are commonly mistaken for actor's verbs (as in those aforementioned lists appearing in other books), but which I believe are actually either results of pursuing several actions or not pursuable without words. To repeat, our *doings* must lie underneath the already written text and become part of the psychological subtext of the character.

to convince—a perceived result
to persuade—can't be pursued without words, therefore becomes
    a perceived result

to avoid—can't be pursued until there is something in the way
　　therefore less useful
to smile—a physical manifestation, not a *doing* in our terms
to cry—an emotional manifestation, not a *doing* in our terms
to undermine—a perceived result of doing several things
to diagnose—cannot be pursued under text
to smother—will result in physical activity or is a result
to undress—an activity, perhaps with the action to fondle, to caress,
　　or to attack?
to enlighten—a result
to build—an activity or a result
to deceive—usually revealed in text or a result
to fascinate—accomplished by multiple actions
to dominate—again a perceived result

There are others that I believe are results of several actions and
are therefore *not* useful enough in the communication to the
actor:

to accommodate
to eliminate
to pamper
to condemn
to empower
to forgive

There are some action words that I would put into what I call the
gray area. They might work some of the time, depending on the
context or the response of the actor, but they often do not elicit a
direct response and therefore one must not assume they can be
relied upon. Words such as

to encourage
to muse
to select
to skirt
to think over
to trap
to glorify

SHORTHAND COMMUNICATION

Often when I was a young actor, a director would ask me to "do more" or "make it bigger." "How much is more?" I would ask myself or how would I make it bigger without making it too big? Many directors are still using these general directions in the hope of getting what they want. There follows a trial-and-error process, much time spent, until finally the director exclaims, "There! That's it." Often a director will say "Can you do less?" But how much simpler and more direct it would be if one were to say "Instead of threatening, intimidate." "Instead of provoke, let's try challenge." Rather than "do more," one might say "instead of greet, welcome." You can see how useful and important it is to develop an extensive vocabulary of these actor's action verbs.

Let us look at the list of action verbs in a different order, one that would replace the "do more, do less" mode of direction so as to give you an idea of their usefulness in playing the instrument of the actor:

to brood	to seethe	to erupt	to explode	
to pose	to strut	to show off	to flaunt	
to caress	to stroke	to fondle	to embrace	
to tease	to taunt	to mock	to "dis"	to put down
to shrug off	to toss off	to laugh off	to dismiss	to reject
to confront	to challenge	to provoke	to incite	
to warn	to intimidate	to threaten	to attack	
to startle	to shock	to amaze	to astound	
to tempt	to tantalize	to lure	to flirt	to seduce
to amuse	to entertain	to perform	to emote	
to check out	to examine	to scrutinize	to probe	

The possibilities are limitless. As you can see, these words can alter the intensity or urgency or lessening of either, increasing or diminishing in a much more specific way than "do more" or "do less." Thus it is necessary for the director to become as fluent as possible with this vocabulary both to be able to identify a doing as it happens organically from the actors' intuition ("I liked it when you shocked her on that line. Keep it in.") or to be able to change intensity quickly ("Instead of shocking her on that line, let's try startling her.").

With the use of this vocabulary of needs and actions we begin to develop the shorthand communication so different from the prose upon which we have been trained to rely. Everything depends entirely on the response of the computer buttons in the actor's brain to any part of this vocabulary. A blank stare or glazed-over eyes in response to any of these words, in terms of both needs and actions, is a signal to the director that the particular instrument with which you are working is not responding and another word or set of words must be found.

Occasionally an actor will say to me "I don't know what that means" when I have just suggested that his life need might be to prove his worth—perhaps his/her particular training dictated the use of a different vocabulary or perhaps there is some form of built in resistance to those words—but then proceed to reveal in the work exactly what I have just suggested. The words have entered the computer in his brain without his conscious awareness and punched up the very response I had in mind. Sometimes the mere utterance of a useful selection of these words will produce the desired results.

This shorthand communication is equally useful in both theatre and film and is particularly useful in television where time is even more of an enemy of creativity. In theatre there are several weeks of rehearsal time in which to explore choices for a character in terms of both needs and moment-to-moment actions. There is also the luxury of allowing the give and take among actors in rehearsal to influence the process of selectivity. The collaboration between actors and director can proceed at a relatively steady pace, thus there is a strong likelihood that everyone involved will arrive comfortably at fulfillment of their individual purposes. In film there is little time to rehearse. Some directors can and will demand a week or two prior to the shoot schedule. Others work right on the set, rehearsing just prior to each shot. Here time is money and every moment counts. This method of shorthand communication serves all forms. It can avoid wasted time and allow the director to help the actor realize the desired vision of the character.

When I directed daytime television we were given 2 or 3 hours of blocking rehearsal for a 1-hour show each day. In addition, directors had to prepare scripts ahead with all shots marked so that the shot sheets could be distributed to the T.D. (technical director) and cameramen. Instead of simply giving orders and making the actors obedient robots in order to accommodate the already chosen moves, my vocabulary of needs and actions enabled me to evoke organic responses from the actors. For example, if I wanted an actor to move away from another actor, instead of saying "walk to your left" I suggested he reject the other character. His response to that word meant he would have to move in the direction that would get the shot. The verb gave the actor the psychological motivation for the move rather than merely responding to a physical direction. The more one experiments with this actors' language, the more shortcuts one discovers. You can see how useful and important it is to develop an extensive vocabulary of these actors' action verbs. **As with the learning of any language, it is important that you become fluent in this vocabulary of actions and needs if this approach is to be useful for you. This can only be accomplished by study and usage**. My students often hang onto the same actors for all their scene work once they've established a working relationship. I urge them to abandon this practice and work with as many different actors as possible, as often as possible. The exercises found in Appendix A are designed to assist in gaining this fluency.

ADDITIONAL LAYERS

This character outline of needs and actions is what I think of as the skeletal bone structure of the character. It is just the beginning of the work an actor must do in collaboration with the director to recreate the behavior demanded by the text. It is the primary work but it must be followed by the addition of other layers such as what follows.

The emotional life both in general as described in the text ("he is a happy-go-lucky guy") and specifically scene by scene ("she has just come from the funeral and is experiencing deep grief").

The physical state of being "She has been blind since birth," as in the play <u>Wait until Dark</u> or for a specific scene, " He has been drinking all night," as in the play <u>This Is Our Youth</u>.

Character adjustments—"His whole character is reptilian," as in the film, <u>Dr. No</u> or "She reminds one of a dumpling," as in the film <u>Bridget Jones's Diary</u>. Some actors like to work with imagery, again sometimes influenced by certain forms of training. Devices such as "I'm seeing everything through a haze of smoke," or "I'm always walking on broken eggshells," or "I have a ramrod up the length of my back" can add a specific layer of character adjustment. There might also be other necessary additions, such as the demand for an accent or regional dialect.

Environmental conditions—Perhaps the character is newly arrived in the crowded big city after living in a small rural community since birth or it is an extremely hot or cold climate, etc.

The development of these layers is an important part of the actors' craft and these elements are also addressed in the actors' basic training. Each actor has his/her own *modus operandi* in the creation of the character, but to be honest I prefer that we collaborate on the bone structure first, i.e., the outline for the character, after which the actor can then add the other layers. This is because I find the actor much less accessible to my suggestions and direction in the shaping of the character if he/she is in the throes of an emotional or physical state and is allowing that state to be the sole moment-to-moment guide. It is incumbent upon the director, however, to make sure that the development of these additional layers is eventually included in the actor's homework, as this will play an important part in the rehearsal process.

PREPARATION AND PERSONALIZATION

It is important for the director to be aware of the necessity of adding these layers to the outline and making certain that what the actor does in his/her homework and is bringing to the rehearsal are compatible with the original vision of the character. It is also essential that with all of these components the actor is connecting organically, not only to the outline, but to the additional layers as well. This often requires that the actor find what we call a **personalization** and/or a **preparation.**

You will remember the exercises I described earlier. I referred to them as useful for a preparation. This means that the actor preparing to do a scene might do a recall of a time when he/she felt a loss of worth as a preparation for connecting organically to the need to prove worth. The actor might do a preparation by recalling a time when he/she felt completely unloved in order to pursue the need to get love. By the same token, if the script called for it, an actor might want to do a preparation for the feeling of extreme heat by doing the recall exercise I described.

What if the actor doesn't feel any particular love for the actor playing the character from which the need dictates he/she wants love? It is then necessary for the actor to personalize, i.e., substitute someone in his/her own life so that he/she can be thinking about that person and the need to get love can become organic.

All these elements, the emotional, the physical, the adjustments, and the environmental, add—to continue the metaphor—flesh, hair, fingernails, and so on to the basic bone structure and contribute to the creation of the whole character. These layers are all part of the actors' craft and homework. If the director is paying close attention and becomes aware that components are missing in the organic realization of the character, it may be necessary to suggest to or remind the actor to do a personalization or preparation for either the needs or the accompanying layers as part of the rehearsal process.

4

The Text and the Throughline

THE TEXT

In the beginning there is the word—and the text is always the beginning for a director. Every choice we make, every character outline, design element, staging idea, and so on derive from the play or screenplay. So the first order of business is to examine the material thoroughly. I have always found that it takes at least three readings of a script to conduct that initial examination.

The first reading should be accomplished as one would read a novel: purely as entertainment and to experience the work without jumping to any quick conclusions or making any snap judgments. Once familiar with the story line, the second reading can provide the opportunity to identify more specific information: the nature of the structure, the genre—comedy, romance, etc.—the characters and how they serve the story. The third reading should enable the director to discover his/her personal connection to the material. What does the director respond to, empathize with, or back away from? During this third reading the director should begin to formulate and even attempt to articulate that which the script communicates to him/her in the overall sense and what might be communicated to an audience with this material.

It is my firm belief that if a director can't relate directly to a script, or disagrees with what the script has to say or doesn't believe the script has value, that director should not attempt to direct that piece of material. It will not only be an unsatisfying experience, it may well turn into a disaster. And I must warn against accepting an assignment and then trying to turn it into something else closer to what *you* want. It is also my firm belief that it is our job as directors to fulfill the intent of the writer as loyally as possible. This is at times an unpopular stance, particularly in the film industry where it is now common practice among the major studios and producers to buy a script and then call for numerous rewrites by a succession of additional writers. The original writer is often ignored or excluded to the extent that the finished product has to go into Writers Guild of America (WGA; the screenwriters' union) arbitration to determine who should get the credit for the final product.

Years ago a writer friend of mine took me to a WGA weekend retreat in the mountains above Los Angeles. Several days were spent listening to the pained stories of well-known writers who were horrified when they discovered, upon seeing the finished films, that their original scripts had been mutilated. As my roots were in the theatre, this phenomenon of the establishment system was a revelation. In addition to necessitating the complex arbitration system, it was one of the motivating forces behind the rise of the auteur in our independent films and the practice of the writer becoming the director.

The theatre, unlike film where the writer is often ignored and the director takes over, gives the writer veto power over everything, as per Dramatist Guild rules. Rewrites cannot take place without the writer's participation and/or consent. Of course, the writer might often, against his/her better judgment, defer to a strong and famous director or a producer threatening to pull the show if certain cuts aren't made. For example, take the original Broadway and traveling productions of <u>A Streetcar Named Desire</u> by Tennessee Williams. The former with Marlon Brando was directed by Elia Kazan with the ending Kazan demanded. The latter with Anthony Quinn was directed by Harold Clurman, came after the Broadway production, and had Williams' original ending restored. Perhaps each director's vision of the whole play was slightly different and affected the choice of behavior for the Blanche character at the end of the play.

COLLABORATING WITH THE WRITER

Since all of our work as directors is collaborative, I feel strongly that the collaboration with the writer should be the starting point. But in order to have a fruitful dialogue with the writer, the director must have his own sense of what he/she sees in the material and what he/she would want it to communicate to the audience in its final form. In order to be able to succinctly express this vision of the material, it is essential to be able to articulate specifically that which begins for the director as a subconscious awareness or a series of pictures in ones' head. However, I believe that the responsibility of the director also must include the realization of the writer's intent. It therefore becomes necessary to find common ground, making sure that ones' vision is compatible with what the writer intended, or getting the agreement of the writer to a somewhat different vision. Thus meeting with the writer to ask questions and have discussions about story line, character, and the writer's vision of what he/she has written is essential.

A question I would put to both myself and the writer in the search for a compatible vision of the material is *"What do you want the audience to know or learn or understand or think about when they're leaving the theatre at the end of the play or film?"* Often one finds that the writer has written mainly from his/her own subconscious and hasn't thought about this at all or, in some cases, doesn't care to think about this. *But the director must have a clear understanding of the what, why, and how of the project. What is the journey? Why are we making the trip?* (or why am I doing this project?). And how do we proceed to get to the destination? You will find that forcing yourself to adhere to the discipline of actually writing down in a sentence or two an articulate expression of what is revolving in your brain in answer to "what is this about for me" or "what do I want the audience to know?" is an invaluable aid to all the work to follow.

"Well," you might ask, "but what if the writer is dead?" This is often the case with plays, particularly those recognized as the classics of the craft. My advice in this instance is to read everything you can find about the playwright or screenwriter, including autobiographies, biographies, other works by the writer, etc. You may very likely discover that the writer has one main theme that appears in most or all of the work and has found many different ways of saying pretty much the same thing. This will provide you with, at the very least, a clue as to the writer's intent in the project you are addressing.

What if the director is also the screenwriter? How does one conduct this dialogue with ones self? My advice, particularly to film school students and many independent filmmakers for whom this is the most common occurrence, is to put the script away in a drawer for a at least a couple of weeks after you've finished the final draft and restrain yourself from looking at it. Then come back to it with the eyes of the director. The writer's process is so different, so much more internal than that of the director who has to lift the words off the page and breathe life and truth into them. It seems to me of utmost importance that the two crafts be pursued separately. Of course, as the project develops, alterations and rewrites may be necessary and the writer or the writer's hat may need to be accessed. But hopefully by that time everyone knows where they are going with the work and the adjustments are in support of the already arrived at vision or journey.

THE THROUGHLINE

This articulation in writing of the director's vision of the total work is what I call **the throughline.** (Again, in other books you may see this word used but in a different context. It usually describes what I call the life need of the character.) In my opinion, formation of the throughline is the most important step in the director's process. If given enough thought and attention in the beginning and shaped to express specifically the director's vision, it can be the guide for most of the choices the director is called upon to make throughout the fulfillment of the project. It can help determine the genre of the work, its structure, and even inform as to casting and design choices. But most importantly it can, in this most collaborative discipline, make sure that every member of the team is on the same page so that all are working on the same play or making the same film. It can become the anchor and the guide when the director is barraged with ideas, suggestions, and questions demanding selectivity. It is insurance that the finished project will turn out to be what the writer and director originally envisioned.

CONSTRUCTING THE THROUGHLINE

When I introduce this concept of a throughline to my classes and ask my students to examine a work and tell me what throughline they might construct for it, the resulting reactions to the material are sometimes startling in their variety. For example, I often assign A Streetcar Named Desire for this exercise. (If you haven't read the play or seen the film, I urge you to do so immediately, not only for the purposes of understanding these examples, but because I firmly believe that directors must be familiar with the classic literature of their craft!)

Here's a response I sometimes get:
"It's about what happens when a nymphomaniac invades a family."

This sentence tells me that it comes from one who believes that Blanche is the antagonist and that Stanley and his wife Stella are on the protagonist side of the storyline. This particular student feels that Blanche is mentally ill and/or a pest and that Stella and Stanley are justified in getting rid of her.

Aside from the fact that I believe this concept is in total opposition to what Tennessee Williams had in mind when he wrote this play, let us examine this sentence as a possibly useful throughline. Does it give a sense of the journey of the play, the structure, or is it more a <u>TV Guide</u> description? I think it is the latter. The throughline as I envision it is very different from a thumbnail description of the story or a pitch line that one might use to sell the project to a prospective producer. It must be a synthesis of what your own gut responds to in the script and what you want to communicate to others, together with that which the writer intends to say. And it needs to be constructed in such a way as to inform both you and your team about:

1. The nature of the characters, i.e., who is the protagonist and who is the antagonist? The protagonist carries the line forward. The antagonist opposes or obstructs the forward motion of the journey
2. Which characters fall on the protagonist side and which on the antagonist side?
3. What is the nature or genre of the material: comedy, drama, political, satirical, protest, etc.?
4. What is the arc of the journey? Where is the high point or moment of greatest risk or major turning point?
5. What specifics can you include that will help your team understand your vision of the material? Period? Location? Political or social background?

Let us look at one possible throughline for <u>Streetcar</u>:

"The sensitive, sexual, poetic romantics in American society of the forties, viewed as misfits and confronted by the unfeeling brutality of those who considered themselves the norm and the others as a threat, were destroyed by a prevailing lack of compassion and understanding."

This provides several kinds of information. It starts with the sensitive romantic (Blanche), and it is her journey that ends in destruction. This tells us that in this vision of the material, Blanche is the protagonist moving the line forward toward the character's ultimate demise and Stanley is clearly the "unfeeling brute" antagonist. It also tells us that perhaps Stella lies in the middle of the structure, leaning toward one or the other. It specifies the period of the forties (things have changed considerably since then, but that is the period Williams was writing about) and also makes it an American story. We might even qualify it further by adding "unfeeling brutality of the blue collar middle class." You can see that there is information for the casting people, the designers, and perhaps even the location manager if you are doing it as a film.

Let us take another American classic, the play <u>Death of a Salesman</u> by Arthur Miller. (Again, run to your computer or your local bookstore if you haven't yet read it.) It is interesting to note that while both these works are period pieces, they still have an amazingly contemporary resonance that enables them to be revived with frequency. They also seem to have a universality, which has enabled them to be successfully translated and performed in many other countries. That is probably why I feel that the best kind of throughline is one that, although specific, can also have a universal appeal. Here again there can be many interpretations of the work. I recently saw a production of this play where the character of the mother was most sympathetic and very much on the protagonist side of the structure. When I saw the original production the mother was clearly on the antagonist side. Miller himself has been known to have made adjustments to his plays to make them more contemporary (i.e., <u>A View from the Bridge</u>) and sometimes small rewrites can change the throughline of the work. Today, many see Willy Loman, the salesman, as a loser, a man who cannot make enough to meet the needs of his family, cannot keep up with the demands of his job, is going a little nuts, has betrayed his wife, and can't seem to relate to his sons. Viewed this way he might actually be the antagonist with mother and sons lying on the protagonist side of the structure. However, if you look at it from the perspective of the period (remember it was first presented in 1949), the work is amazingly prescient. Willy Loman is the last of a dying breed: the small, independent, self-starting businessman who is being swallowed up by the younger generation of growing corporate cartels and sprawling supermarkets and is victimized by the growing national hunger for material possession. Arthur Miller was indeed a prophet of sorts.

So in the latter vision the throughline might be something like:

"The small individual businessman in his desperate attempt to fulfill the myth of the American Dream personified by the amassing of material wealth is dooming himself to eventual eradication."

On the other hand, taking a different approach, the throughline might be something like this:

"The individual who desperately pursues the myth of the American Dream as a symbol of his worth and virility may be depriving those dear to him of the things they really need and ultimately planting the seeds of his own destruction."

As we study a script we bring to it our subjective perspective based on who we are, past experience, generational factors, and a host of other considerations that will determine what we as individuals perceive the material to be in its totality. Whatever the director chooses to make of the material at hand—and it is entirely his/her decision finally—**this self-imposed discipline of actually condensing ones' thoughts and transferring them from the subconscious to the conscious level by writing them down, translating them into a useful and articulate sentence, is in my opinion the most important part of the director's process**.

It is the crucial first step. Our work is so entirely collaborative and there is so much input from a variety of sources as we travel along the road to completion that we are always in danger of losing our intent for the finished product. The constantly arising demand for careful selectivity and the ensuing dilemmas in both theatre and film about who to cast, what to revise, what to cut in the play, or how to edit the film can be helped immeasurably by a well thought out, carefully worded throughline, which provides a solid base to which we can constantly refer.

How often have you seen a play or a film and been bored to the point of dozing or dazzled by fast-moving images that don't seem to add up to something comprehensible? How often have you seen a play or film that goes in one eye and out the other so that mere days

later you can barely remember it? Of course, there are many elements that can endanger the successful fulfillment of a project: weak
script, faulty casting, poor editing, an incompatible music score, a
poor support system, etc. But taking the time to do this work on the
construction of a useful, durable throughline is to me a kind of insurance against falling into the traps that lead us to disaster. In addition
to being a constant reminder of the *raison d'être*—that which motivated you to take on the project to begin with—it can be the anchor
throughout the many phases of preproduction, production, and, in
film, postproduction. That is, providing you have taken the time to
give it enough thought and have been able to construct this sentence
or two with what I call the *buzz words*. The *buzz words* are those that
help transfer the pictures in your head to the heads of your team.
For example, in the throughline for <u>Death of a Salesman</u> referred to
earlier, I consider "desperate" one of those words, as it gives us a
sense of the high stakes. "Myth" may be another. Certainly
"American Dream" conjures up images. "Doom" and "eradication"
have a dramatic intensity that signals serious or even tragic drama.

Of course the throughline doesn't have to be a heavily
weighted or a philosophical or social treatise. It can be something
as simple as "Everyone should have a good laugh as often as possible and we are going to make you laugh at the human comedy."
The important thing is that you know what you want the audience
to be thinking when they leave the theatre.

If I sound like an adman in my repeated attempt to sell you the
concept of a throughline, it is because I see it as a step in the work
regrettably often overlooked or bypassed. It is true that construction
of the throughline is the hardest part of the director's work and
surely the loneliest, most introspective part of all that we must do.
Everything after this step involves other creative and supportive
members of the project team. I call it a team because it is essential
that each individual working on the project becomes part of a whole
unit that moves as one toward a common goal. I like to think of our
work as much like that of a conductor of a large orchestra. Each
musician is an expert in the playing of his particular instrument. It
is the conductor who interprets the piece of music, making all of
these individual artists' efforts into one sound as he/she shapes the
finished work. In order to get the desired result there must be
mutual understanding of what that goal is. In other words, everyone—actors, designers, producers, and assistants in every area—
must be working toward the same end. This is as true for theatre as

it is for film. If you believe as I do that creative input from the members of your team throughout the project is a much needed asset to the director, then you can appreciate the importance of the communication of this common goal. Too often seemingly constructive suggestions offered with the best intentions can throw the project into an entirely different direction if the director hasn't taken the time to firmly establish his vision for himself and with his team. A carefully thought out and well-articulated throughline that clearly expresses your intent, while difficult to arrive at, is worth all the effort.

"ORDINARY PEOPLE" AS PROTOTYPE

There is an Academy Award-winning film by a first-time director that often provides a good prototype for use in my classes and at this point I urge you to view it immediately on VHS or DVD so that it is fresh in your mind as we progress through the next pages. It is particularly well suited for our purposes because, in addition to being the work of a first-time director, it is a small canvas, actor-driven film. The film is Ordinary People (1980), directed by Robert Redford. It is an old chestnut to be sure, but because of its universality, clarity of line, and fine performances by the actors, it holds up amazingly well.

If one looks closely at the opening sequence in the film, a surprising amount of information about the director's throughline can be gathered. Look at the first few cuts of the film. If you put them together with your awareness of the story line, you will see that Redford is, through the choice of shots, giving you clues about his throughline.

First there is a shot of a body of water—the place where the accidental drowning happened, the place that supplies the underlying emotional line. The camera moves toward the dock from which the two brothers presumably departed with their boats. Next we see trees. A forest? No, very quickly we know that it is a park, as the grass is neatly mowed. The falling leaves follow and tell us that the season is fall, but also remind us subliminally of death as we see all those dry dead leaves on the ground. The cement paths and roads signal not an urban or rural setting, but that of a distinctly suburban milieu. This awareness is confirmed by the appearance of a gazebo, which begins to inform us that this might be an upper middle class environment. Next we see a church, which appears to be other than Catholic—perhaps it is more Protestant in form. The following shot of the high school continues to be consistent with the images of an upper middle class suburban environment. If you have any doubt about Redford's intentions thus far, the director then pans the faces of the class engaging in choral practice. The homogeneity is startling, not a distinctly ethnic or minority face in the crowd. These students are all white, mainly Anglo Saxon, and possibly even Protestant. Very shortly after we've received all this information, the director lets us actually see the license plate of the parents' car and we know that we are in Illinois, i.e., middle America. All of these signals lead me to believe that Redford's throughline must have been something like this:

> *"The White Anglo-Saxon Protestant ethic so prevalent in upper middle class middle America, which dictates repression of feeling and the preservation of the mask of perfect conformity, will result in the destruction of the family structure. If caught in its grip, one must find a way to release one's self from this constricting repression."*

Bear in mind that the whole opening sequence as described is entirely the director's choice as to how to begin his film. There is no dialogue and no sound except the mood-setting music of a single piano, also the director's choice. I think it is interesting to look at who the director is in this instance, what Mr. Redford's own background might have been and how the response to his own gut might have influenced his choice of this material and his throughline.

In the theatre as well, information or a particular mood can be conveyed at the very start of a play by what the director chooses to show the audience in terms of setting, lights, sound, music, and activity, which may or may not be provided by the actual text. This is where the creativity and imagination of the director enter into the mix. And the throughline is the guide and the anchor.

WRITING THE THROUGHLINE

There are many ways to pursue this construction of a throughline. Many of my students find that it takes a few days or a few weeks of thinking and mulling over and rewriting these all important words to get them to be concise, articulate, readily understood, and useful. Remember that you are going to share this with your team so it goes beyond what you yourself already understand. Let me suggest one way of accomplishing this task.

1. Read the script at least three times.
2. After the first read, which should be purely for familiarizing and enjoyment (hopefully!), as you go through it a second time begin to write words in the margin of the script. These words should be whatever occurs to you at that moment either from your reflexive response or from your subconscious. Let yourself free-associate. The words don't need to make any particular sense. Just write whatever comes into your head.
3. When you've finished this reading of the script, look at the words you've written and see if there is any continuity of thought or if these words seem to lead you in a particular direction. Then add any other words you think pertain to either the story line or development of character.
4. Try to compose a trial sentence or two using some or as many of these words as are helpful.
5. On the third read, test the usefulness of your throughline. Does it describe the journey? Does it identify the inherent obstacles to the forward motion of the journey? Does it give you information about the structure? The characters? The locale? Will it help you make choices of needs for the principal characters? Will it get everyone on your team on the same page?

The next time you go to see a film or a play, try to construct what you feel was the intent of the director. As you leave the theatre, see what you can identify as the throughline of that director. At times it is very difficult, as many directors don't bother with a throughline and simply sew together scene after scene, faithfully (or sometimes not so faithfully) rendering the text to tell the story that lies therein. Many films of late are what I call "in one eye and out the other" experiences, i.e., those that one forgets a half an hour after seeing them. Plays often have more depth, but sometimes it is difficult to identify the author's *raison d'etre* for writing the play. It can be motivated by the need to express a howl of pain, an excising of guilt feeling, or a blow-by-blow narration of the coming of age process, perhaps making the director's construction of a through-line more difficult. It is my firm belief that if all writers and directors could collaborate on the articulation of the what and why of the work, we would have infinitely better and more fulfilling results.

One more observation prompted by my presence at a recent screening of a small-canvas buddy film that has garnered a great deal of attention called <u>Sideways</u> (2004) directed by Alexander Payne. This film about two men friends on a week-long vacation in the wine country of northern California has a cast of four principals, a handful of smaller day player roles, and a small group of ensemble players. The press kit I was handed at the screening listed under credits the cast, crew, designers, technical and production personnel, and all others that had a hand in getting this film completed and into theatres. In this relatively small, low-budget people film there were 300 individuals on this list.

Out of curiosity I looked up a theatre program—<u>Playbill</u>—to get a count on a Broadway production. The number of individuals involved totaled about 150 for a straight play. A musical production would probably involve at least twice that number. As director your task is to make that imposing and diverse number of individuals into one team all intent on helping you realize your vision.

If you do this throughline work carefully and constructively, you will have an aid in that task, a point of reference at every turn, an anchor, and a guide as you labor to bring the pages of your script to life.

Analysis of Script

5

GENRE

Now that you have armed yourself with the security of a throughline, the next step is analysis of the script. That is, the examination of the text for information regarding genre, structure, the *givens*, etc. Let us start with genre. Is it a comedy? If so, is it farce (i.e., the film <u>The Three Stooges</u>, the play <u>Noises Off</u>) or satire (i.e., most Tom Stoppard plays or the film <u>The Player</u>), comedy of manners (Moliére or Noel Coward), or the comedy of situation and character (Neil Simon)? Is it drama, i.e., tragedy, mystery, horror, domestic drama, etc.? If it is a screenplay, is it fast action (<u>Fast and Furious</u>), heavy on hardware (<u>Terminator</u>), or more reliant on special effects than interpersonal relationships (<u>Men in Black</u>)? Is it experimental (plays by Samuel Beckett), avant garde (plays by Eugene Ionesco), stream of consciousness (plays by Sam Shepherd), or old fashioned in structure (Tennessee Williams)? Is it highly stylized (Shakespeare) or naturalistic (Arthur Miller)?

Here again, the answers to these questions can be determined either by the nature of the material or by the director's choice. I've seen naturalistic material turned into highly stylized farce (sometimes unintentionally alas!) and vice versa, with varying degrees of success. In any case, the choice must be made at this stage of the work as it will affect all the steps to follow: casting, design, character outlines, etc.

You might even want to look at the words in your throughline and alter them slightly to better communicate to your team your perception of the style of the work. This doesn't imply the necessity of changing the nature of the journey, but simply the manner in which it is conveyed. Remember, we are looking for the buzz words that will connect to the computer button/brains of the members of your team.

STRUCTURE

Further analysis of the script should reveal the writer's structure. As directors we are essentially storytellers using the recreation of human behavior in order to tell our tale. In the case of the play form, the structure is most often conventional. It is a one-act, two-act, or three-act form, with the more period pieces usually written in three acts and the more contemporary work using the two-act structure. However, many of the more contemporary playwrights have chosen to break that mold. Their free-form, sometimes stream of consciousness style mimics rock music; they play at a certain intensity until they've come to the end at which point they seem to simply fade away. Most screenwriting classes also address the development of a script with a kind of three-act sensibility: first act, the set-up and introduction of characters; second act, the development of plot; and third act, climax and resolution. And yet here too there are ways to break the convention, either in the way the script is written or in the way it is ultimately edited for the finished product. For example, the quirky structure of the screenplay for the 2003 film 21 Grams written by Guillermo Arriage was faithfully preserved by director Alejandro Gonzalez Inarritu.

Most often the director's choice prevails when it comes to the dramatic structure of the play or film. Taking into consideration the length, scope, and shape of the original script, the director must decide on the elements that will enable him to construct what I call the *arc* of the journey. Sometimes it helps to think of the journey of the throughline as a mountain climb, with the mountain peak corresponding to the climax or major turning point. By the same token, I think of each scene along the way as a station on the journey. Thus, in attempting to design for one's self the structure of the play or screenplay, the first thing to look for is the top of the arc in the overall sense. Where does it all seem to hang in the balance? Where is the major crisis? What is the turning point? What are the stations along the way? What are the obstructions to reaching the top? Then, again starting at the beginning, what is the arc of each scene and how does it further the progress of the climb?

POSITION OF CHARACTERS

After defining for one's self the nature and arc of the journey, it will then be easier to determine the position of the characters in the structure. Who carries the line forward? Who seems to obstruct the forward motion? It is your throughline that will lead you to the answers to these questions. *The protagonist carries the line forward; the antagonist obstructs it.* The leading characters will be easier to identify, but you must choose for all the characters. Knowing what side of the structure they fall on is key to all the choices that follow. It is also interesting to note that not all characters fall on one side or the other. Some might stand squarely in the middle in the ful-crum position. Some might cross over from one side to the other in the course of the journey. The design of the structure is essential in the director's process of selectivity.

THE ARC

Using <u>Ordinary People</u>, a small canvas domestic drama, as the pro-totype once again, let's reexamine the possible throughline we've suggested.

> *"The White Anglo-Saxon Protestant ethic so prevalent in upper middle class middle America, which dictates repression of feeling and the preser-vation of the mask of perfect conformity, will result in the destruction of the family structure. If caught in its grip one must find a way to release ones self from this constricting repression."*

This indicates that the protagonist is the character who is caught in the web of the WASP ethic and that the arc of the story is deter-mined by his struggle to break the bonds of repression. This also tells us that all who assist him will fall on the protagonist side of the structure and that all who cling to the ethic and resist his efforts will fall on the antagonist side of the structure. It is then pretty easy to find the top of the arc. It surely must be the scene with the psychiatrist in which the protagonist manages to gain his release from the gut-wrenching repression. Starting from that point and working backward, we can then track the development of the journey toward the release, with all the pitfalls along the way. If you examine the material scene by scene you will see the attempt at the beginning to cover up, to hide emotion, to conform to the expectation on the part of all characters. Gradually there is an attempt by the protagonist to relieve his distress, and the outsider is introduced in the person of the psychiatrist. This outsider begins his arc toward effecting the release of the protagonist as he assists the climb to the climax.

You will also be able to identify the obstacles that confront the protagonist along the way in successive scenes with the mother, father, grandmother, peers. *In creating the structure, it is of prime importance to identify the obstacles, as they provide us with the antagonist side of the structure. It is conflict that creates dramatic action. Without it, we have what I like to call a flatliner.* There is no arc in a flatliner, merely life happening, which condemns us as the audience to an experience akin to watching paint dry or, at the very best, a kind of sterile voyeurism.

A good illustration of the building of this arc scene by scene can be observed by viewing each Conrad/Psychiatrist scene in succession. You will see that in the first few scenes together the director keeps the two characters separated either physically or by choice of shots. There is a table between them or they are kept in what we call *singles* so that we view them separately. The light is fairly high. As the scenes progress and Conrad gets nearer to his release, the lighting grows darker and more intimate and the two characters are brought together in *two-shots*, which get tighter and tighter as we approach the top of the arc and the intensity grows. All the elements—character development, design, lighting, music, editing, etc.—can contribute to the shaping of the overall arc of the work and the individual arcs of the scenes.

In the theatre the director can build the arc with performance, staging, pacing, design elements, and music as well. The film director can accomplish much in the editing process. He/she can control what the audience sees by what shot he/she selects to show them at any given moment. The stage director must have sufficient understanding of the fundamentals of stage craft to be able to lure the eye of the observer to where the director wants it to be at any given moment. The director must also be able to collaborate with the cast and with the designers so as to structure all acting and design elements in the shaping of the arc of the play.

This planning of the structure of the play or screenplay is as important a part of the preproduction work of the director as the creating of the throughline. The more homework of this nature a director can do before meeting with actors for the first time, the more security and trust will be generated with the team. Too often I see beginning directors wait for the inspiration provided by the team. They put off the necessary homework until they've received a certain amount of input from their cast, designers, and others involved in the project. I'm a firm believer in the necessity of full collaboration, but I feel strongly that the director must be at the helm of this journey and thus must have a firm idea of what is to form the nature of the destination and the route by which it is reached. Actors will tell you that they want a director who is **prepared.**

The primary need of the actor is a sense of security, provided by the knowledge that the director will protect him/her and help make the performance as good as possible. "It's my rear that's on the line, that's up there on the stage or screen—you (the director) are long gone" is how the actor thinks. The director who can combine and balance a sense of leadership and guidance with a generous spirit of collaboration is one who will engender the highest level of security and trust among the actors on the team.

THE GIVENS

In all of the director's preproduction homework the choices are guided by the *givens* in the text. By that I mean that which the writer has given us as fact about the story and its characters. Sometimes the writer provides a great deal of information about the backstory, i.e., that which occurred before the action of the script takes place. This can provide details about the characters' earlier lives and perhaps explain how they got the way they are when we first see them. This is extremely helpful in this phase of the work. In the event that there is little information of this nature, it is necessary either to meet with the writer and ask the relevant questions or, in the absence of that option, to work with the actors to create the back story and character histories. Sharing with the entire team whatever unwritten scenario and details you create is of primary importance.

Let us go back to the prototype, <u>Ordinary People</u>, and examine the givens in the script.

1. There has been a death by drowning. It has had an impact on the three remaining members of the family in different ways.
2. The family members are typical contemporary upper middle class residents of suburban Lake Forest, Illinois.
3. The missing member was Conrad's older brother, who was the apple of his mother's eye.
4. Conrad at 16 is in high school, a member of the swimming team, coping with the adolescence-to-manhood syndrome, and devastated by the loss of his brother whose drowning he witnessed and tried but failed to prevent.
5. Mother is still grieving and unable to communicate with her remaining son, but tries to maintain the mask of normalcy both with family and with others.
6. Father cares about his wife and son but seems at a loss as to how to deal with their grief and his own until things get so bad that he has to seek help.
7. Conrad's recent past includes an attempted suicide in an effort to alleviate the pain of his survivor guilt. He was sent to a psychiatric facility for a short time.
8. In his attempt to return to some kind of normalcy, Conrad seeks help from a psychiatrist who happens to be Jewish.

And so on. The givens are everything you can glean from the text that will help you make the choices that will steer your course on the journey.

Let's look at the throughline again:

"The White Anglo-Saxon Protestant ethic so prevalent in upper middle class middle America, which dictates repression of feeling and the preservation of the mask of perfect conformity, will result in the destruction of the family structure. If caught in its grip one must find a way to release ones self from this constricting repression."

Armed with our analysis of the script in terms of genre (drama), structure (the top of the arc is the Psychiatrist–Conrad scene in which he releases his real emotion), and the givens, we are ready to proceed with the next step. We must analyze the characters and determine their positions in the text as we begin to make choices for the outlines of the characters.

The Character Outline

6

PROTAGONIST OR ANTAGONIST

Remember, when I refer to the character outline it is in regard to the specific choices of life need and scene needs made in order to identify and plan the character's behavior for the entire length of the journey in the text and in your throughline. Taking into consideration the work described in the previous chapter, it is now necessary to examine each principal character in terms of his/her position in the structure.

1. Does the character fall on the antagonist or protagonist side? (The protagonist side includes those making the journey or aiding in the climb to the top of the mountain. The antagonist side includes those who attempt to obstruct the climb.)
2. Who carries the line, goes on the journey, or moves the story forward? (Who is the main protagonist?)
3. Which character or characters stand in the way of the forward motion of the protagonist? (Who are the antagonists?)
4. Which characters seem to lie in the middle of the structure, between the two opposing forces?

This determination of the position of the characters in the overall structure of the work is an important part of the director's responsibility. This is not a burden to be placed on the shoulders of the actor. The actor must breathe life into his/her character—lift the words off the page and turn them into a living, breathing human expression. The director is the one with the overview of the whole and therefore it is he/she who must attend to the design of the structure as a whole. It is my belief that this determination must be made before the casting process can begin, the reasons for which you will discover in the next chapter.

Referring once again to our prototype throughline, it seems clear that Conrad is our protagonist. He is the one who seems to be trying to escape the bonds of repression and conformity. Who then is on the antagonist side of the structure? Who is clinging to the conformity and continuing to repress emotion at all costs, including the preservation of the family? The Mother is the obvious choice and perhaps the Grandparents fall on the antagonist side as well. What about Father? His position in the structure is interesting; he does not seem to fall easily on one side or the other. He seems to be intent on pulling the two sides together and staying in the good graces of both. So where does he fit? Let's look at the throughline again:

> *"The White Anglo-Saxon Protestant ethic so prevalent in upper middle class middle America, which dictates repression of feeling and the preservation of the mask of perfect conformity, will result in the destruction of the family structure. If caught in its grip one must find a way to release oneself from this constricting repression."*

The Father's journey seems to start smack in the middle of the structure. He is torn by loyalty to the antagonist but feeling the pull toward the protagonist and gradually works himself over to the protagonist side by the end (with the help of a visit to the psychiatrist).

You'll notice that I keep repeating the throughline. I think it's important to examine it at every turn, at every step of the selection process. If it is to be your anchor, you must keep it constantly in the forefront of your brain.

ANALYSIS OF CHARACTER

Armed with all of the necessary information, i.e., genre, overall structure, the givens, the throughline, and the position of the characters in the structure, we are now prepared to begin the process of selection of the characters' outlines. Bear in mind, however, that everything in this stage of the process is to be written in pencil, not written in stone. That which we arrive at in this phase must be tentative until we've had the opportunity to collaborate with the actor playing the character—a topic we will discuss in the chapter on the rehearsal process.

Now let us look at the character of Conrad, our choice as the protagonist. What words in the throughline give us a clue as to the possible life need choice for the actor playing this part? His journey is described as a "release from repression of feeling." Conrad is clearly suffering under the burden of preserving "the mask of conformity" to such an extent that, as we know from the back story, he has tried to do away with himself as a means to alleviating the pain of his grief over the death of his big brother. But is it grief that is the operative word? We also know from the givens that he agonizes over the fact that he tried to save his brother and couldn't. Is his need to destroy himself? No, that can't be it, because the character actually seeks help in the person of the psychiatrist. Remember, we all have all these basic needs all the time. It is that which is **placed in priority and pursued from the very beginning to the very end** that ultimately decides the behavior of the character in any given instance. It would seem that something stronger than the need to relieve his pain by destroying himself must be his priority.

MAKING THE CHOICE

Let me refer you to the list of basic needs on pages 23–24. Do you see anything there that might be a choice? What is the feeling Conrad tries to repress and strives to get rid of? Yes, you've got it, I'm sure. The life need that seems most operative, that seems to be pursued from the very beginning to the very end of the characters' life in the script, is **to get rid of guilt**. When we first meet him he is attempting to sublimate the guilt and then he attempts to release himself from its clutches through the contact with the psychiatrist, through his rebellious interaction with mother, and further interaction with his former friend from the hospital, his new girlfriend, and, finally, his father.

Let's go to the Mother character. We've decided that she's on the antagonist side of the structure. Referring to the list again we see that there are several possible choices that at first glance might fill the bill. Since she is trying to preserve the "mask of perfection," we might look at some of the hold-on-to needs: Hold on to security perhaps?

But wait: she opts to leave the family at the very end so that can't be the choice. And see how destructive she is to her remaining son. What is causing her to be almost brutal in her relationship to him and his distress? Why must she leave when challenged by her husband? That too seems quite self-destructive. Well, we seem to be moving toward the word destroy in the life need of the Mother character. Would the choice be to destroy one's self or others? Not quite. In this case I think we need to be more specific. I would choose to identify it as **destroy the pain**. Her means of doing that involves denial and preservation of the illusion of normalcy and perfection. This could cause her to ignore or block out Conrad's turmoil. The role is difficult and complex and one that could evoke either hatred or sympathy for the character depending on the moment-to-moment choices of director and actor. In Redford's version, Mother was so clearly antagonist that it was easy to dislike her. How could she be so cruel to a son so obviously in at least as much pain as she endured? This was clearly a directorial choice that we'll return to in the chapter on casting.

What about Father, the man who seems to be in the middle? Can you pick out a life need for that character? What do we know about him? He is the moderator, the ameliorator, the one trying to bring the protagonist and antagonist together. Is the need for security his priority?

Well, if that were the case, how can we justify the last scene in which his honest confrontation causes Mother to leave. What does he say in that scene? "I don't think you love me anymore." I would opt for the need **to get love** as the priority life need for the Father character. This need for love is often found as the priority in characters who lie in the middle of the structure. They neither move forward nor obstruct; most often they try to bring the individuals they love together. Their primary mission seems to be understanding, love from all and peace.

The fourth principal in this small-canvas film is the psychiatrist. On which side of the structure does this character fall? His task is to midwife the release of the protagonist, therefore he is clearly on the protagonist side. But we have no back story for this character as his entire purpose revolves around his work in his office. Therefore I would choose the need that focuses on the work: **to prove his worth**. If he succeeds in helping Conrad he will have proven that he is valuable and good at what he does.

Once having determined the structure and position of the principals, the smaller roles fall more easily into place. For example, the character who becomes Conrad's girlfriend is on the protagonist side, whereas his friend from the psychiatric facility places herself on the antagonist side, as she surrenders and commits suicide, making Conrad even more guilty and almost sending him into a threatening tailspin.

The Grandmother and Grandfather are clearly on the antagonist side. I call subsidiary characters such as these *foils* to the main protagonist and antagonist.

Bear in mind that there is always more than one possible choice and that the **choices must take into consideration service to the throughline, as well as service to the actor creating the character**. It is essential that this consideration of selection of life needs for the principal characters takes place before the director begins the casting process. This information will prove invaluable as it becomes necessary to make the final casting decisions.

Let's take another example to analyze. Remember the possible throughline for Death of a Salesman? Here it is:

> *"The small individual businessman, in his desperate attempt to fulfill the myth of the American Dream, personified by the amassing of material wealth, is dooming himself to eventual eradication."*

It seems clear that Willie Loman is the protagonist in this throughline. What might we choose as the life need for the Willie Loman character? Look at the words "desperate," "dooming," and "eradication." They signal extreme urgency and perhaps the use of the word "save." What other words can lead us to a choice? Look at the words "individual" and "businessman." They imply that the need relates both to the protagonist himself and to his work. A man's sense of worth is certainly tied to his success or failure in his work—thus I would lean toward **save his worth** as a possible choice of life need for Willie. This choice would serve right to the end as Willie apparently commits suicide in order to provide his family with insurance money when all else fails. It is the only means left of being of some value. (You'll notice I often qualify a choice with "perhaps" or "possibly." That is because at this point, as I've said, all choices are written in pencil and await the process of collaboration with the actor playing the role.)

Who lies on the antagonist side? According to the throughline, it is those characters who embrace the myth of the American Dream. This would certainly seem to include the Mother who, if you recall, yearns for the material elements that would make her world complete. What might we choose as a life need for this character? Perhaps it is **to get security**, as it seems that she feels she needs the possession of these material things in order to ensure the health and safety of her family.

Where do Biff and Happy fit in the structure? Protagonist or antagonist? Again it becomes a directorial choice. Do we want the audience to identify with them, root for them, or dislike them? In the throughline we are using as a prototype, it would seem that Happy falls in the middle, much like the character of the Father in <u>Ordinary People</u>. He is constantly trying to mediate, ameliorate, and get everyone to like him. The life need choice would appear to be **to get love**, just as it was in the centrally located Father character.

Biff is a bit more complex. He seesaws back and forth between the two conflicting sides. He is a character in conflict searching for where he belongs. The search would lead me to the word "find" and the "where he belongs" would steer me toward **find his identity** as a possible life need choice. However, you might think that this character has another priority before he can even begin the search for identity. Do you know what I'm thinking about? It might be **to free himself** from his father as a priority choice.

So you see, much of the shape of the work and the design of the characters is open to directorial choice. Imagine the power in the hands of the director! You literally have the ability to make of the material what you will. Hopefully what you make of it is compatible with what the writer intended. Your choices depend on your analysis of the script, your throughline, and your vision of the shaping of the characters. But remember they must also depend on the actors with whom you are working. Because all these words and phrases I've used are means of connecting with the actor's brain/computer and eliciting the behavioral responses that you hope to see. You will find that I continually remind everyone of the importance of this aspect of the approach. If the actor doesn't make a connection to what you are suggesting, you are simply blowing bubbles in the air and of little use to him/her or yourself. The collaboration with the actor in the search for a useful choice of needs must continue until you are both satisfied.

Let's look at <u>A Streetcar Named Desire</u>, which was a play and a film (surely you're familiar with it by now!). Remember the possible throughline?

"The sensitive, sexual, poetic romantics in American society of the forties, viewed as misfits and confronted by the unfeeling brutality of those who considered themselves the norm and saw them as a threat, were destroyed by a prevailing lack of compassion and understanding."

(As stated previously, because the work is a period piece, this throughline is in the nature of a look back, whereas when it was first performed the throughline would have been stated in contemporary terms.)

It is clear that Blanche is the protagonist as the perceived romantic misfit and that Stanley registers unfeeling brutality toward the protagonist and lies on the antagonist side of the structure. Where does Stella fit? Once again we find a character in the middle, trying desperately to hold on to both sides. With this throughline, what would you choose for the life need of the Blanche character? Well, because the word "destroy" appears, it seems that **to save herself** might be the choice. By the same token, Stanley would probably have the need **to get rid of** Blanche. If you wanted to make the character even meaner, you might choose **to destroy** Blanche (which in fact he succeeds in doing, as she is carried off to an insane asylum). What about Stella? Well, in this case the character's priority need might not be to get love—it might be **to hold onto security**, as she collaborates with Stanley to get rid of Blanche in the end. Another choice might be **to hold onto Stanley**. Whatever the choice of life need, it must be able to serve the actor for the entire length of the script, from start to finish.

It is important to remember that when suggesting words like those just given that in all probability your actor or actors aren't personally familiar with anyone named Stanley or Blanche. Their craft will dictate the necessity of the *personalizing* to which I've referred, i.e., making a substitution from their own life experience. They would have to, for example, use a recall of someone they wanted to either destroy or hold onto in their own lives.

You will notice that I'm using examples from the literature of both theatre and film. That is because so much of the preparatory work of the craft of directing is the same for both forms. Later on we will discuss the differences. But I feel that both the craft of the actor and the craft of the director in both theatre and film involve all of the same steps in the process thus far.

7

The Casting Process

The next step is perhaps the most challenging, the most time-consuming, and often the most important part of the director's work. Mike Nichols, the great stage and film director, has been known to say that he believes it is 85% of the work. At times it can be mystifying, arduous, entertaining, bewildering, and/or intensely frustrating. Because it is all these things and more, I feel that we must be as prepared as possible in terms of what we seek. The more structured we are in the way in which we go about trying to find exactly the right choice, the more satisfactory and productive the end result will be. Of course there is always a degree of luck involved, as well as the possibilities of certain imposed restrictions that are beyond the director's control: budgetary limitations, the demands of a producer or a studio in terms of packaging or marketing requirements, such as star names or a gaggle of actors attached to an agency involved in the picture deal, or the demand of an investor who has a "talented" niece who wants to be in the theatre, etc. Sometimes it becomes necessary to make painful decisions, such as eliminating the choice of a friend or former collaborator for a role or withdrawing from the job altogether if the demands coming from other participants in the project are so outrageous as to jeopardize your ability to stay true to your vision.

THE CHARACTER DESCRIPTION

In any case, *it is imperative to have a clear idea of what you want to find before you begin the casting process.* All the work described in preceding chapters should help you arrive at this. Do not, under any circumstance, believe that it is best to wait until the character as you've visualized him/her walks in the door of your office with the right height, the right color hair, the right "look."

I'm reminded of an experience I had as the casting director of the Mark Taper Forum in Los Angeles many years ago. In my consultation with a visiting director I was cut short as I attempted to ask the questions that I thought would help define the character and assist me in providing him with a list of people to see. "Just keep 'em coming, honey," he said. "I'll know it when I see it." Well, in truth he didn't have a clue and the process was long, arduous, and ultimately unproductive.

CASTING RESOURCES

Of course, casting for a student film or a workshop or off-off Broadway production of a play lies at one end of a broad spectrum of possibility, with the other end being a Broadway show or a multimillion dollar film. In the latter situations there are ample funds for a very efficient and knowledgeable casting director who can do much of the spade work. Sometimes even a low budget or a low-low budget student project will spring for a hired casting director to help streamline the process.

The first step is the lining up of the actors who might be right for the roles. There are a variety of ways to accomplish this. Advertising in the trades, i.e., <u>Backstage</u>, the New York trade paper, or <u>Dramalogue</u>, the Los Angeles trade paper, or on the union call-boards, i.e., Screen Actors Guild (SAG) or Actors Equity Association (AEA) is one way. Advertising is often used by directors of student films, showcase productions, and other low- or no-budget projects. There is also a service called The Breakdown Service, which sends a list to agents of the casting needs of many current projects in both theatre and film. There used to be reference books often used by casting directors, such as <u>Player's Guide</u> published by Equity and <u>Academy Players Directory</u> published by SAG that listed pictures and contact information of many actors (but not all) by category. However, now only the SAG directory is accessible and probably used less than the resources provided by Internet sites such as Google Directory-Arts.

CATEGORIES

And then there are the files of casting directors and agents, which are also sometimes maintained by category. These files are usually the result of years of experience and attendance at many auditions, showcases, off-Broadway plays, and independent films, as well as the usual sources. Happily, casting directors now get well paid and well credited.

Let us examine what I mean by categories. The conventional, and with the contemporary blurring of lines, somewhat outmoded, classification might be as follows:

Juveniles, male or female—children from age 7 to 15 or so
Young Leading Man—age 16 to 24 or so
Young Leading Woman—age 16 to 23
Leading Man—age 24 to 50
Leading Woman—age 23 to 45
Character Man—age 50 and up
Character Woman—age 45 and up

Sometimes there is more definition to the classification, i.e., Character Comedian or Young Character Male.

ARTICULATING THE DESCRIPTION

Although these standard categories are used less and less because there is so much crossing over, it is helpful to identify for the casting director or the Breakdown Service the category that your search involves. What is really needed is a specific and articulate description of the role you're trying to fill. This is where the process frays for many because the usual descriptive paragraph is often so general that it might well imply the inclusion of just about every actor in America. Let me give you an example of what I mean with a sample of a typical paragraph:

> *"Seeking young attractive male to play part of neurotic, depressed, artistic character in a Chekhov play titled* The Seagull.*"* (Haven't read it? Again, I send you to your local library!)

The ad is for the part of Trepliov of course. What actor of any age wouldn't think of himself as able to play "young" and "attractive?" Also, what actor worth his salt wouldn't think of himself as able to play "neurotic," "artistic," or "depressed?" The result of this generalized ad would be hundreds upon hundreds of responses, either with gluts of the pictures we lovingly call 8×10 glossies or phone calls and emails if you've been foolish enough to give out that information.

Then hours of time go by as 40- and 55-year-old men of varying weights and ethnicities file in to be seen. Alas, the ego of the actor! What a waste of our time and theirs (and let me remind you that time is money in our business).

So the first step is to master the art of writing the character description for the casting director, the breakdown service, or the ad in such a way as to maximize communication and minimize unwanted response. Here is where the concept of *specificity* becomes of primary importance.

Let us go back to our prototype, <u>Ordinary People</u>, and the role of Conrad. What are the words that would bring in actors who are as close to the right type as possible? Well, let's start with "high school student, must look 16" (Timothy Hutton was, I believe, in his twenties when he played the part, so we don't need to say "must *be* 16"). Perhaps "competitive swimmer." (This would eliminate the grossly overweight, hopefully.) According to our working throughline, we might also use the words "Caucasian" or "Anglo Saxon." This can be a sensitive area. I am a firm believer in what Actor's Equity calls *nontraditional casting*, i.e., casting with disregard as to the color or ethnicity of an actor as long as that actor is capable of playing the role. (There is a website for Equity's nontraditional casting project at <u>www.ntcp.org</u>). However, because this script clearly calls for a specific segment of our society, it is only fair to save the time of the minority actors too visually specific as to be useable. Because we can't use someone with a Brooklyn accent, we might use "middle American environment." (If they have an accent but can lose it successfully because they are wonderful actors, we don't want to automatically eliminate them.) We also need to signal to the casting directors and agents the size and demand of the role so I would include the words "young lead." So the ad for Conrad in the Breakdown Service or trade paper might be something like:

> *"Casting young lead in family drama. Anglo Saxon student in middle American high school must look 16 and be a competitive swimmer."*

The important thing to remember is that the more specific facts you can supply and the less descriptive prose you include, the more likely you are to slim down the process and enable those that are assisting to be of constructive use.

CASTING DIRECTORS

After completing this chapter on casting, it occurred to me that it would be useful to hear current attitudes from casting directors who are presently working in both theatre and film so I interviewed two New York City-based casting directors, asking them what they did and did not want to hear from a director. It was startling to find how similar their responses were and gratifying to learn that we were all in complete agreement on certain key points of the process.

Liz Woodman

"I want to hear what the director wants, what the director's vision is for the piece as well as for the specific characters. I can tell the director what I think I want but I'd also like to hear your take and your ideas so it becomes a collaborative process. Not that I would ever impose—I can't. My job is to serve the director, the writer, and the producer—to find the people that they want. But the director needs to be specific so you have an idea to go on and then you can go from there. In film or theatre there can easily be specific physical or plot requirements. For example, I did a show once where the leading man was 6′4″ and he said 'I want the person who plays my daughter to be at least 5′7″ because I don't want to look down all the time.' If you have a short leading man you might not want Nicole Kidman. You need to think of proportions. If the whole plot hinges on a character having 'x' characteristics, you need to know that. And also there are the emotional qualities, the range of an actor. If you really need a physical quality maybe you could compromise on the emotional or vice versa or the range of talent, which is probably a little more applicable in film where you might be able to get away with a lack of range of talent because you could make up for it visually. For me, the talent is always what you're looking for.

"I have a file but I would put it on the breakdown service, which goes to all agents and get people in that way. Then, if the producer has the money, have screening auditions where I and sometimes the director's assistant will sift through 400 people. I don't keep files much anymore as they get out-of-date, but I do keep all my audition notes.

"A director I don't want to work with is one who says 'Oh, I don't know. I'll see it when it walks in the door.' Also someone who is *so* specific that there's just no leeway, no realization that maybe for this project you're not going to find somebody that's available; maybe if it's a low budget, or a play being cast during (TV) pilot season. At some point, when you've seen people and have trusted your casting director and the casting director says in a polite way 'I've sat through a week of general auditions, you've seen five days worth of people—this is it.' You have to be able to accept that.

"I also don't want to work with directors who are not kind and understanding to actors in the audition process. I find that there are a lot of directors who don't really like actors. If they treat them well, then the actors are going to show well. They're there to help you and it's a collaboration. And if you're nasty to them or not encouraging, especially with an actor where it's all behavior and instinct and all those things that you want a good actor for, if you are not encouraging then you're not going to get results because they're going to close down. Another thing that annoys me is when the director can't really tell. If the actor is totally wrong for the project, thank them, keep their picture in a file so you can keep them in mind, and tell them goodbye.

"I have actors do a scene from the material and I get good actors to be readers. If you have a really good actor being the reader it helps the audition and I like to use material from the project. I sit in on all the callbacks. Actors Equity limits the callbacks to two plus the first audition for regional theatres. For Broadway principals it's three callbacks and for Broadway chorus it's two.

"The bottom line is that auditioning is one of the more unnatural processes—whether it's a kid or an adult what you have to do is make them comfortable. Casting directors can make it as comfortable as possible, but one of the main responsibilities, I think, of the director is to make the actor feel 'I can do that—I'm being supported. I'm going to expose myself emotionally and I can do that better if I feel there is support from the other side of the table.' We're safe: we're sitting behind the table. They're out there, which I think is so brave. Know what you want, be open, be kind to the actors, and be supportive."

Judy Henderson

"I want to hear as exactly as possible what the vision of the piece is and each character: their qualities and an age range. I don't particularly like descriptions like "she should be blond and 5 feet tall" and that kind of thing because when you're that visual you take away all of the qualities that an actor can bring to playing the part and you have a prescription. So yes, you'll find someone who is 5 feet, who is blond, and weighs 110 pounds but the ultimate question is can that person act? And if possible I'd like a director, if he or she could, to get a little past the 'me' part because that's always the part that they're very keyed into visually—the 'me' part in the piece that is most like the person and so you're trying to replicate a human being as opposed to having the performer bring qualities to a part that could be a little different and much more interesting. Example: A while ago, when we did Other People's Money, the writer had a vision of the lead character Garfinkle who was 6 feet, a big man visually, imposing and he could not get past that. And I did a production of it out of the city with a really good actor who was visually what the director saw. When the piece came to New York, that actor was not available and we saw a number of people. There was one actor that I thought was the perfect embodiment of this character, although he was 5'7" and redheaded and had no relationship to the visual description of the character. It got to a week before rehearsals with no Garfinkle and I said 'please, why don't you see Kevin (Kevin Conway).' He came in, they fell in love with him, he created the role, and he has become the standard for the part. In fact, when the film was made, Danny DeVito played the role. And the play was a great success, played for several years Off-Broadway. I have a letter from the author, complimenting me on my idea. But when you're so closeted and so close to the vest about a visual view, you totally close up creativity.

"I'm pretty open to what a director's vision is. After all, it's my job to service the director. I think when you're given sides to audition actors I think that they shouldn't be the whole play. And we're in a situation now where the director, who has done a lot of work, has given us three scenes—43 pages to give to an actor to prepare for an audition. It's ridiculous because she will get very little of what she wants and if she gets anything it's in spite of what she did. It's counterproductive. I think it's better to choose part of a scene because very often when you see an actor auditioning you know with the first several lines whether that person is in the world of the piece or not. The rest is just self-indulgent.

"I sit in on most of the sessions. I think the power of the casting director can be more negative than positive. If I feel very strongly about something I will voice it but I have to be very careful the way I do that because I think directors like to feel that this is their creation, especially if they're confused and they can't decide between one character and another character. You very often find that a strong sell on the part of the casting director takes a negative turn. I find if I say this person is terrible the director will listen to that. If I sell a person, they'll be put off sometimes. So I try to talk about the positive aspects of each of the people they see and point out the differences that casting that particular person will bring to the piece.

"I don't find any difference between theatre and film in terms of the casting process. The difference is in how the actors audition because theatre is much broader and more physicalized and, consequently, a theatrical audition for a film piece doesn't work. Also the language is very different. Theatre is the medium of the language and film is the medium of the visual. Consequently less is more in film and in theatre you really have to be able to use language well.

"I sometimes bring a camera in, depending on the film. We often tape the callback. I like the initial audition to be free. Once you put a camera there you're limited to sitting in a chair so I think it can limit the actor's ability to find character qualities. But in a callback situation it's important to know that you can get an actor who can sit still. I think there should be a limit on callbacks. People become too self-indulgent. In SAG you have the initial audition and then one callback, which is enough, especially if you have the person on tape.

"If a director has a relationship with the casting director, that director really opens himself up to finding more interesting and talented actors."

READING THE 8×10'S

In the event that you don't have a casting director or assistant to do the preliminary work for you, the next challenge that presents itself is the weeding and winnowing of the usually enormous pile of 8×10 photos you are sure to receive even with all this care taken to reduce the load. This necessitates learning how to *read not only the*

*picture, but, more importantly, the back of the print where the actor pres-
ents the bio.*—all of the vital statistics, such as height, weight, con-
tacts, and experience and training.

Unfortunately, often much of the information on both sides
might be a lie; a white one, indeed, but misleading nevertheless.
Pictures can be retouched, hair styles change, and actors don't
always update their head shots. You may be looking at a 10-year-old
picture. A strong, macho-looking head may be attached to a 5 foot
body, which may be just what you want, but be careful not to make
assumptions about the total visual look of an individual from the
head shot alone. As for experience and credits, actors often must
invent or enlarge upon their histories with the awareness that a
dearth of experience spells doom to the job-getting process. After all,
how do they get a start if they don't create some background in the
early stages of their careers? I never fault an actor for getting creative
about the experience. Once, however, an actor looked me straight in
the eye and told me he'd been in a play I'd directed. I'd never seen
him before in my life. I'd be less inclined to hire him, not because he
lied about his history, but because he didn't do the necessary
research on who I was and what I had done. This told me that he was
a lazy actor, one who didn't bother to do his homework and was
more likely to rely on the impulse of the moment than to invest in
preparation. Because that is not the kind of actor with whom I enjoy
working, I would be most likely to pass on him.

An 8×10 is usually laid out as follows: Name at the top, followed
by union affiliations: AEA, SAG, and AFTRA (American Federation of
Television and Radio Artists). All phone numbers, agent information
if the actor is represented, and usually statistics concerning weight,
height, and sometimes coloring are next. Experience, which is often
called Credits, follows and is usually organized by classification,
i.e., film, theatre, television, commercials, and industrials. These are
listed in columns by title, role, or type of part played, producing
organization, and director. The next heading is Training, which usually includes academic as well as professional or conservatory listings,
such as New York University Tisch School of the Arts, BFA in Drama
or The Ensemble Studio Theatre, or The Stella Adler School, or a list
of individual acting teachers with whom the actor has studied. Last
there is usually a heading of Special Skills such as sports, i.e., horse-
back rider, swimmer, black belt, etc. as well as other languages
spoken, dialects and accents the actor is able to deliver, and any other
special accomplishments.

UNDERSTANDING THE TRAINING

Often the information that I consider the most informative is what appears under the heading of training. Over the years I have discovered that I have more of a rapport with some actor-training approaches than others. This kind of selectivity is completely subjective and based entirely on both my own prior experience and some understanding of what current approaches involve. I believe it is the responsibility of the director to become familiar, or at least conversant, with various contemporary techniques and methods (you'll notice I use a small *m*!) so as to be able to communicate with each actor in his/her own language. As we progress I'll discuss how to evaluate the actor's ability to respond to your communication and how the actor translates it in terms of his/her own technique. At any rate, when I look at the actor's bio. and see, for example, that the actor has had some form of Meisner training (Sandy Meisner, former head of the Acting Program of the Neighborhood Playhouse and founding member of the Group Theatre), I'm usually favorably inclined. This is because my previous experience with Meisner-trained actors has always been very positive; they are flexible, responsive, and action word oriented. When I see that the actor has studied the Strasberg approach or been trained at the Actors Studio, I'll know that I'm likely to get a different kind of response—perhaps intuitive, moment-to-moment, improvisational, emotionally based, etc. There are excellent books on both the Meisner and the Strasberg training techniques with which I would urge you to familiarize yourself.

There is a big difference between putting together a play with 4 weeks of rehearsal and shooting a film with a much tighter and more structured time frame. The particular needs of the project at hand will influence choices of actors in addition to the budget for the project. The knowledge of what to expect in terms of training can provide a useful guide. Thus it is valuable to learn about current teachers and their approaches so that you can process the information the actor has supplied under the heading of training. Many acting classes allow observers and it is also useful to take an acting class or two whenever you can fit it into your schedule to add to your understanding of the various training techniques.

Another helpful piece of information is the name of a director or two the actor has worked with in the past. *If one is seriously considering using an actor it is important to reference check, just as one would do with a corporate position.* Only in this case you would want to check with a former employer/director and ask the relevant questions: Did the actor do the homework? Did the actor get to rehearsal on time? Does the actor have any problems we should know about, i.e., substance abuse, alcohol, volatile temper, etc.? Did the actor take direction? Did you enjoy working with the actor? There are always going to be surprises, but the more you can learn up front, the better armed you will be to make the right choices.

It is sometimes helpful to look at other information the actor has chosen to include in the bio. Is the actor athletic? Does the actor speak more than one language? Does the actor do dialects? What is the weight and height?

The experience and credits listed are often the least important information on the back of a head shot when deciding if you want to take the time to see that individual. I would give training and reference contact a much higher priority. In any case, at this point you might be able to eliminate a good number of the 8×10's with which you've been deluged and selectively arrange for those who seem possibly suitable to come in for an interview.

Yes, I do firmly believe that *an interview is a necessity as both an aid to the process and a time-saving device.* It gives the director the opportunity to study the whole of the actor's instrument, including vocal equipment, perhaps discover any idiosyncrasies, and further pursue the weeding out process so that once again you are not deluged by the obviously unsuitable in the ensuing audition period.

THE INTERVIEW

The interview actually begins at the moment the actor steps through the door of the office or rehearsal space. **I strongly advise against holding any phase of the audition in anyone's home**. It is not only potentially threatening, particularly to women, it risks surrounding the project in an aura of unprofessionalism. Spring for the extra few bucks and rent a space if necessary. *Watch how the actor enters*: What is the body doing? Does the actor strut in or seem to timidly tiptoe? Does the actor wait to be told to take a seat or does the actor hurl himself into the nearest chair? Does the actor look at you or at anything but you? What is the posture of the actor? (I remember James Dean, the actor famous for <u>Giant</u> and <u>Rebel Without a Cause</u>, in the early days when we were all job hunting together, always looked as though he were walking against the wind, head down, shoulders hunched.)

How does the actor sit in the chair? Is the actor proud of his/her body or attempting to hide it? If he/she had prior information about the character, what did the actor choose to wear for this meeting? In other words, *study* the actor intently and learn all you can about his/her instinctive behavior even before the conversation begins. In this way you might get a bead on how close the actor's own persona is to the character you are casting.

There are a few specific questions that will often give you the kind of information you are seeking besides the obvious "what have you done lately?" For example, "What role have you played that gave you the most satisfaction or fulfillment?" "What director did you enjoy working with the most?" "What director did you not enjoy working with and why?" Granted these are general questions, but perhaps the actor will reveal something that will let you know he/she is either ideal for you or entirely wrong for you. If, for instance, you are the kind of director who relies heavily on improvisation and the actor lets slip that he/she loathes improvisation, or vice versa, you have learned something important about the potential of the relationship. If the interview seems to be going well, you might want to ask more specific questions based on demands in the script, such as do you have any siblings, have you ever lost a member of your family, or how is your relationship with your father?

There is also something to be learned about the actor from the questions that the actor might ask or from the fact that no questions are asked. Is it that the actor is timid, or is it that the actor doesn't want too much input from the director. Perhaps it is that the actor plans to rely on the impulse of the moment. Again, all these possibilities are signposts about the nature of the instrument you are interviewing.

In sum, during this phase the director must add the role of psychologist to all the other directorial skills in observing the instincts and behavior of the actor. Why should this be necessary? I hear you thinking "Isn't it enough to see, hear, and talk to the actor to decide whether I want him to read?" Well, perhaps. In terms of this approach, however, wouldn't it be wonderful if you could find the actor who not only looked and sounded right for the character, but also had the same or a similar life need as the one you've chosen for the character or, at the very least, some frame of reference or emotional connection to the specific demands of the character? Then you could really trust the actor's instinct and intuition as being appropriate for the character and much of your work is done. It is for this very reason that I believe that the *work of forming the throughline and deriving from it the possible life needs of the characters is an important preliminary to the casting process.*

This is where your constant study of human behavior in all its complexity pays off. In observing the actor during the interview in the way I've described earlier, insight into the actor's needs might be gained. If you are casting a shy, withdrawn character and the actor seems naturally aggressive and outwardly directed, it will be a test of the actor's skill and craft to create a totally different mode of behavior. This is not to say that one should turn one's back on that actor necessarily. Certainly there will always be the DeNiros and Streeps who seem to be able to assume the skin of any character as though it were their own. But to be forewarned about the degree of difficulty the actor might face in the recreation of the character's behavior is a definite aid to meeting the challenge of the collaborative process to follow.

Referring again to our prototype, <u>Ordinary People</u>, I'm reminded of the amazement expressed in the film community when Mary Tyler Moore, long established as America's sweetheart as a result of her popular television series, was chosen by Redford for the role of the cold, repressed mother. But possibly the director knew some facts about the actor that others didn't think to factor in. There had certainly been some pain in Ms. Moore's personal life: perhaps a divorce, the death of a son, a physical condition that was not revealed publicly until later in her life, and the necessity for maintaining a public persona gave her ample emotional resources upon which to call.

GRACEFUL REJECTION

One of the most challenging hurdles for the new director to overcome is learning how to reject someone gracefully and in the least hurtful fashion. Unfortunately, for people in our profession, rejection is too often the name of the game. Thus actors must learn how to cope with constant rejection for the most inane of reasons usually having nothing to do with their ability (too short, too tall, too dark, too thin, too intellectual, etc.) and inure themselves so that they can continue to function without too much loss of self-esteem. It is such a difficult demand that many fall by the wayside specifically because of this aspect of the profession. I have seen less talented people who have the drive, determination, and the skin of a rhinoceros stay the course and eventually succeed because they stuck it out long enough, where much more talented and sensitive actors have been forced to drop out and choose another path. (Oddly enough, I know more than a few who selected the field of psychology as an alternate choice of career!)

Some directors seem to feel that if they string the actor along with a "we'll call you" or "I'll let you know" even though they know they don't want the actor, they are postponing the inevitable pain. Others find it is easier to say "Thank you" and let it go at that, leaving the actor guessing as to how he did or what might happen next. Having been the daughter of an actor and an actor myself, I can tell you that you are doing no one a favor if you go this route. The actor's time and energy are just as important as yours, and nothing can be accomplished if one is hanging onto the phone and hoping for a call. Remember that often it is the actor's livelihood, rent, or next meal that might be at stake. And if this job isn't the one, they need to be able to have that information as quickly as possible so they can plan their next move. **So please don't leave an actor hanging if you know that you aren't going to hire him/her**. Give a simple "Thank you very much. I'm sorry we can't offer you anything at the moment. But perhaps there'll be something in the future we can work on together." This last is a carrot to let the actor know that it wasn't a total disaster. Of course if it was a disaster and you really want to get this actor out of the business, the "thank you" can be followed by "there's nothing for you in this project." Try to avoid the prefaces of "I'm afraid that . . ." or "I don't think there's anything. . . ." These leave room for possibility and it is cruel to give an actor hope when there is none. It is difficult but much kinder to be truthful.

As for those in whom there is interest, it is at this point that I like to give the actor a copy of the complete script if at all possible, an indication of what scene or scenes to prepare, and a time and date for the audition. I'm often asked why I don't do the whole thing all at once: give the actor the script and let him read right then and there. It is because I really don't believe in what we call a *cold reading*, which is a reading without any preparation on the part of the actor. For me a *cold reading is simply a test of the actor's elementary school education and can't reveal enough about the way the actor works or what the actor might bring to the role beyond what is on the page.* Therefore I like to give the actor at the very least a couple of hours or perhaps overnight to read the whole script and make some choices for the character. In this way I'm given the opportunity to observe the actor's imagination and creativity as well as the interpretation of the role. If you are very short on time or can't afford to get the audition space for more than 1 day, I suggest you give the actor the script and provide him/her with a quiet corner for an hour or two. This would of course require that you interview in the morning and read in the afternoon.

My advice at this point is that you answer any questions the actor might have about the part, but avoid getting too involved in a dialogue about needs or anything else that would amount to the beginning of direction. It is best to wait and see what the actor comes up with to get a full measure of capability and compatibility.

THE AUDITION

In my opinion, no matter how limited the budgetary resources are, it is imperative that you have someone other than yourself present to read with the actors. There is no way that you can fully concentrate on the reading when you are participating yourself and are forced to look at the page rather than at the actor. By all means, supply the actor with someone who can be responsive, i.e., another actor, as opposed to a stone-faced or monotone stage manager. It might be necessary to pay for the use of actors in readings, but sometimes another member of the project will fill the bill gratis. However, I believe that it is important to see how the actor *reacts* as well as how he acts so it is important to have him/her play with someone who can give the actor something to which he/she can react. If it is too difficult to get an individual with whom all the actors can read, then I would advise choosing a scene for two characters and sched-uling actors in pairs so they can read with each other. This puts more pressure on the director who will be forced to study both actors simultaneously during the reading, but it is less negative than the alternatives.

Try to select the audition material wisely. Prepared monologues, the ubiquitous tool of many in the current audition process, provide me with little that is constructive. In the first place, monologues force the actor to relate to an unseen or absent entity, creating a false circumstance. In addition, the monologue has perhaps been worked on and over and often coached by another individual so that what one is seeing is the actor's response to another's direction rather than his/her own creativity. Actors usually slave over their repertoire of monologues but I always feel that is a hard way to put the actor's best foot forward. In fact, I often tell actors that I believe that the monologue audition was invented by people who want to get actors out of the business! Therefore, select a scene from the play or screenplay that you feel will reveal the actor's craft as much as possible. However, avoid choosing the climax scene or the most hysterical or high action demand. Those can be saved for the final choices after you've done more weeding out from the list of those you've lined up for the reading.

In this time of advanced technology, the temptation to bring a camera into the audition process is strong, particularly in casting for film. After all, it is an opportunity to record in detail and not have to rely solely on one's memory. It is an option and up to individual choice. However, my preference, even in casting for a film, is to wait until a later stage of the process when one is down to the last few candidates for a role. The presence of a camera can be very distracting, both for the actor and for the auditioner. In addition, more time must be spent in the viewing of tapes of a large number of actors who, in your mind, you might already have rejected as a result of the reading. Also, the stationary camera might miss some of the more subtle, behavioral moves the actor might make, thus eliminating valuable information, particularly in casting for theatre.

THE FIRST READING

In the audition process as in the interview, I believe it is important to *watch the actor like a hawk from the moment of entry into your presence*. The more you can learn about the actor's instrument, the easier the choice will be. Careful observation is the best way to educate yourself.

Before or during the reading the actor may have questions about the role or about the script as a whole and I have no problem with answering them, within limits. You may find that some actors like to delay the actual audition as long as possible. As stalling does not serve your purposes or help with your time constraints, I would advise a certain amount of patient response and then a simple request to start the reading.

Do bear in mind that auditions are an extremely stressful situation, both for the actor and for the director. The actor is thinking about advancing his/her career, which is a life-determining factor or perhaps paying his/her rent or even being able to eat that week. The actor must also deal with the issue of self-esteem and the potential for embarrassment or, even worse, humiliation in the audition process. The director is thinking about whether the right people can be found for the parts so that the carefully arrived at vision will be fulfilled successfully, whether he or she will be allowed to work again after this project, or whether the critics, both journalist and self-styled, will embarrass or humiliate. It is, at best, a loaded situation.

Thus *respect* becomes a key word in the process. It is so important to maintain an awareness of how you are treating one another in this difficult process. Lack of respect breeds at the least annoyance and at the worst anger. Uta Hagen, the late renowned and brilliant actor and acting teacher, called her first book Respect for Acting. My plea might be the sequel: respect for actors! You must remember at all times the difficulty of the actors' craft; the necessity of figuratively (and sometimes literally) stripping naked in the process of mining parts of themselves, which they must then expose and reassemble to recreate the behavior of the character. One of the reasons I encourage directors to take acting classes is so that they can viscerally experience the process and develop a compassionate awareness of the degree of difficulty with which actors ply their craft.

Directors who participate in such things as *cattle calls*—the amassing of large groups of actors for open call general auditions, which necessitate hours of waiting to be seen—are, in my opinion, exhibiting a callousness and lack of respect that are totally counterproductive. It seems to me that the little that is accomplished is hardly worth the negative aspects of such an endeavor. Remember, everyone else's time is as valuable as yours.

By the same token, the scheduling of both the interview and the audition should be carefully thought out and arranged in such a way as to prevent the necessity of causing a lineup of anxiously waiting actors. It is important, particularly for film directors, to have a carefully defined sense of time and to learn how to organize the tasks and apportion the time appropriately. I must confess that with all the negatives associated with directing for television, particularly in the area of never having enough time and the necessity of constant compromise as a result, I personally found that the lessons of budgeting time, so essential for our process, were of enormous value.

There is nothing more draining for an actor than a long waiting period. This is true not only for the audition process, but also for a film shoot. The endless hours of waiting for the technical aspects to be put in place, particularly lighting, can leave the actor exhausted and hardly ready to do his/her best work. Knowing how to handle these long but usually necessary waits without getting stale or spent is the mark of the true professional. (I remember years ago how impressed I was at the enormous repertoire of word games that the actor Lee Grant regaled us with on the set of <u>The Landlord</u>. It taught me a great lesson about how to keep oneself alert and occupied.) Therefore, in the audition process it is essential to be very organized and to keep a weather eye on the clock if you want to see the best work of the actors you've called in.

It is important to help the actor relax and feel comfortable once the reading begins if you want to see his/her best work. I always feel that actors are like sponges. You have seen in earlier chapters how the actor must sharpen his/her sensory perception as an essential part of their craft. This means that they are trained to hear and see everything and that they will pick up your vibes if you are tense, dismissive, or simply reacting to your own indigestion. Actors are also self-involved of necessity so they will assume that everything negative that they are sensing relates to something they are doing wrong. Because tension reduces the blood supply to the brain, a tense atmosphere will stand in the way of your seeing the actor's best work. Despite the demands of time, the urgency to find the right casting, and the fatigue and boredom that set in after hours of enduring less than interesting readings, *it is incumbent upon the director to maintain an open, pleasant, relaxed, and, if possible, welcoming atmosphere*. This includes introducing the actor to those present at the reading and of course to the person with whom the actor will be reading the scene.

I do like to supply a chair for the reading, but encourage the actor to move about if so desired. Actually I like to see what the choice will be as it often reveals how comfortable the actor is with movement or how the actor feels about his/her body. During the reading I watch for the actor's ideas and selectivity. Does the actor find an interesting counterpoint choice that perhaps I hadn't thought of—or does the actor simply make the lines sound natural?

Does the actor listen to the other actor or person who is reading in the scene? Does the actor bring the character to life in the way that you envisioned—or does the actor have a take on the character that is not yours but is equally interesting? What you should be doing at this point is not necessarily looking for the immediately perfect fulfillment of your vision for the character, but rather for the actor with the physical resources, skill, talent, and craft to follow your direction and collaborate with you to realize and perhaps even enhance your vision of the character.

After the first read through a decision must be made. Are you interested in this actor or do you know immediately that it isn't going to work? If it is the latter, then again the simple and direct response is the only option. Do not let the actor hang, thinking there is a possibility of a callback when you know there isn't one. Thank the actor for his/her time and let him/her know that although you enjoyed the reading, the actor is not right for the character as you see it.

If the first reading is interesting and you think the actor has potential as a candidate for the part, at this point I feel you must find out about another important aspect of the process. *How does the actor respond to direction?* Give the actor a simple direction and ask that he/she try the scene again. It doesn't even have to relate to the script. For example, tell him/her that this time he/she has to go to the bathroom very badly but doesn't want the other person to know. (Some call this addition to the character *an adjustment*.) What you want to see is if there is a difference between the first reading and the second one. If the line readings are the same, this would indicate that the actor had prepared the scene but can't depart from the previous choice. Once the actor gets glued to a line reading it is something like being stuck in cement and it is unlikely that he/she will be able to respond to your direction and your shaping of the character. *The evaluation of how well and how quickly the actor receives and incorporates direction, specifically your direction, is to me one of the most important steps in the audition process.*

THE CALLBACK

At the end of this initial process you will no doubt have narrowed the list of possibles considerably. Advancing to the next step, usu-ally designated as the *call-back*, should include selecting one or two additional scenes to be read, again always informing the actor ahead of time so you can see the results of the actor's preparation. Once again, you must have someone ready to read with the actors. At this point you might consider matching actors. If you are looking at actors for the role of the mother, for example, you might want to bring in candidates for the role of the father to read with them. Some directors like to wait for the final few to do this matching, but scheduling actors in pairs at callbacks can sometimes help both time and budget.

During the callback reading there are specific clues to identify:

1. Does the actor seem more relaxed in your company?
2. Does the actor respond to the reading partner? React to differences in the prior reading?
3. Has the actor brought any new ideas for this reading? Has the character grown since the first reading?
4. Can the actor's physical and vocal traits fulfill your vision of the character? Be careful here. Remember that makeup, wigs, and prosthetics can do miracles so don't reject a marvelous actor without careful consideration even though he/she doesn't quite fill the bill physically.

And, of course, above all, *if you are really interested, work a bit with the actor*. Although I don't go into throughline or specific needs and actions choices even at this point, it is useful to try out a directorial idea or two just to see and evaluate the response. However, take care that any discussion or direction is not so extensive as to be perceived as picking the actor's brain for new ideas. That should only happen after the actor is hired!

For example, let us say you are auditioning for the role of Conrad in <u>Ordinary People</u> and you have chosen the first scene between Conrad and the Psychiatrist. After hearing a first read to get the actor's ideas—remember, this is a callback—you might suggest to the actor that he try it again and include the adjustment that he really doesn't want to be in this office with this man. If, however, the actor has already brought that element into his reading initially, you might suggest adding the sense of guilt he has about his brother or some other adjustment that wasn't present in the first reading. In other words, use a little more time to find out how flexible and responsive the actor is, because no matter how talented, this is *your* project and you need the actor's collaboration with *your* vision.

On occasion you may run into a special consideration or specific problem with an actor. Older character actors might resist taking direction from a younger or first-time director. Some actors also have directing background and may reflexively add their two cents to the mix, particularly if they feel the director is less than totally prepared. Some men resist taking direction from a woman. Some actors work very slowly and have to gradually process a direction so the immediate response might be misleading.

In regard to this consideration of the way in which actors work and respond, I'm reminded of an experience I had on a project that starred the legendary Maureen Stapleton. Watching this gifted actor was not only a privilege, it was a class in itself. At the first rehearsal she listened and responded to others but the character was almost a blank page. With each ensuing rehearsal a new layer appeared. Gradually the character became fuller and more complex until finally we were all dazzled with what she had created. It was like watching one of those fast-action films of a bud growing through stages to become a rose. Of course in such an instance, where there is a history of fine performance, one doesn't need to worry when the first reading seems flat. Suffice it to say that, in general, a director's response to the actor's audition must be tempered with patience, intuition, insight, and wisdom. In some cases, what you see is not always what you get.

CASTING CHILDREN

And then there is the question of auditioning and casting children. Here there is such a wide range of possibility that the topic almost requires a book of its own. Each age presents a different set of circumstances and demands adjusting of the approach to the particular child. And within the given age or age range there are tremendous variables, often depending on the environmental and parental influences brought to bear. Even the head shot can be misleading as children tend to change physical appearance in a matter of weeks. The age at which children are able to read and comprehend varies enormously. The individual attention span is also a huge variant.

With very young children who cannot read, improvisation and game playing are required. Here again, it is a question of using your intuitive perception in order to assess the nature of the child: outgoing or withdrawn? Verbal or silent? Secure or challenged?

From age 7 and up, most children can read, have a developed personality, and can be auditioned with the actual script using some or all of the techniques described earlier, particularly the investigation in regard to taking direction. Here you want to find out how the child responds to authority, how creative the child seems to be, and how long the attention span is. Most importantly, try to determine if the child is having a good time or if the whole experience appears to be an obligatory chore.

This brings up the most important aspect of casting children: *Cast the parent!* Ideally you should look for a parent who either drops the child off and asks for a pick-up time or is content to wait in an adjoining room. If the parent hovers or pleads to be allowed to watch, I consider that an alarm bell. If the child comes in already knowing the lines, complete with line readings, having worked over the script with the parent ad infinitum, I consider that an alarm bell. Children learn very quickly and tend to get sing-song if over-tutored. If the parent appears tense and seems to feel that there is a lot at stake, I consider that an alarm bell. Undue influence on the child makes me suspicious of the parent's motives in allowing the child to become an actor. Is it self-fulfilling ego, financial need, or just a new fun experience for the son or daughter? How much pressure is being exerted on the child? It is necessary to evaluate and attempt to predict what the parent's behavior will be during the shoot or on the set because it can make all the difference in terms of time, the attitude of the child, and the possibility of a positive relationship between you and your little actor.

The callback reading is your opportunity to learn as much as you can about what pitfalls might lie ahead with your casting choices. If you remember, I did warn you about the necessity of assuming several roles: parent, conductor, philosopher, psychologist, etc. This is the stage where the psychologist hat is most useful. So often have I heard a student bemoan a disastrous casting choice after we have screened a less than successful project. It usually goes something like "The reading was so great, but then when we got on the set he turned into an enormous pain in the ass!" Since few of us are clairvoyant, we can only hope to protect ourselves from unwanted surprises by being as astute as possible during the audition process.

In the theatre if a mistake is made, there can be the opportunity to salvage the situation. Some Actors Equity contracts include what is known as the just cause clause. And there are among the myriad types of contracts ways of making changes if necessary, sometimes

involving contractually specified payment. A change is often designated as "artistic differences" in the press release. Because firings
and withdrawals can be costly, do not help the general *esprit de corps*,
and tend to fray trust at any stage, the option should be regarded as
a last resort.

In film, however, it is much more difficult. Unless you have been
able to negotiate or schedule a rehearsal period before shooting, you
are forced to either grin and bear a casting error once principal photography has begun or raise the budget considerably with reshoots.
This is one of the reasons that I feel that a 1- or 2-week rehearsal
period is mandatory for a feature film shoot. Even with that as a
buffer, you may have to deal with costly contract issues if you feel
you must replace an actor. In student and low-low budget films there
is such a limit on the time frame of the schedule that replacement
is rarely an option. Thus it is incumbent upon the director to use
as much care and time on the casting process as on location hunting,
storyboarding, etc. Too often, particularly in student films, I find that
the process is left until the last minute and, of necessity, is condensed
or even rushed to the detriment of the end result. Another factor that
film students must grapple with is the fact that often actors used in
their projects are not paid and must drop out at the last minute to
accept paying work. One can hardly blame the actors, but it does
leave the filmmaker in a terrible hole. For this reason I always advise
students to have a back-up plan for the principals; perhaps the runner up to the first choice in the final audition. In sum, to avoid disaster, enough time must be allotted, the schedule of appointments must
be organized carefully, and the director must pay close attention
using sensory perception, instinct, intuition, and a reservoir of
knowledge of human behavior as well as the actors' craft.

MAKING THE FINAL CHOICE

Presumably after the callback, you will have whittled the list down
to the final few. I have little patience with those directors who find
it necessary to call actors back in time and time again because they
can't make up their minds. Aside from the fact that the actors'
unions may have specific rulings about this, I feel it reveals a lack
of preparation and an indecisiveness on the part of the director. It
sends the message that the director doesn't know what he wants
and is going on a protracted shopping trip.

ADDING THE CAMERA

It is at this point that the camera might be introduced into the process. Although it is not always necessary in theatre casting, it can serve as a memory jog when you are down to the wire in making the final choice. Certainly in film casting it is a necessity. In addition to using the final callback to work further with the actors and help in the final selection process, you want to cut down on unfortunate surprises that only the magnifying glass of the camera might reveal.

For example, at one point we were attempting to cast an 8-year-old boy for a demanding part in a short film. We were about to settle on one very gifted lad with whom everyone fell in love immediately. And the attending parent behaved perfectly. Alas! We discovered when looking at the tape that the child had a nervous squinting eye tic that we hadn't even noticed in the readings. On camera it became a major distraction and, sadly, we had to choose a less gifted but more workable child for the role. One needs to protect oneself from unwanted surprises. The only surprises we want should come from the creativity of the actor in the process of recreating the behavior of the character.

MATCHING AND CHEMISTRY

As noted, another important element to address at this point is that of matching father and son, mother and daughter, lovers, siblings, etc. Again particularly in film, matching can make your task easier. In the theatre, physical matching is not that much of a concern. The distance the proscenium provides allows for much leeway in this area, but certain physical considerations must be addressed in both cases. Actors of considerable size, either vertically or in width, might present specific problems.

Then too there is that ephemeral element called chemistry. Not long ago after what I thought was successful casting for a play I discovered during rehearsal that the leading woman and leading man had been former lovers. Although I had picked up on the chemistry, I was unaware of any negative history. Fortunately, both actors were talented and professional and didn't allow their history to interfere with the process. But mishaps of their earlier relationship could have led to a catastrophe. Don't expect revelations of this sort from your actors, but keep your ESP sharpened!

Unfortunately, there are inevitably those times when, for a variety of reasons, you are forced to accept choices over which you have little or no control. In the theatre there are often financial considerations affecting decisions: the agent demands too high a salary or—the old cliché—one of the big backers insists on the hiring of a friend or relative. In television, often the executive producers or the *show-runner* (formerly known as the line producer) might make the casting choices and it is up to the director to do the best he can with the already assembled cast. In film, often the director is presented with a *package* put together by the agency or the studio that needs to fulfill prior commitments, which might include stars, featured players, and so on depending on the budget of the film. This situation often confronts the director with a dilemma: Should one do the job with actors one doesn't believe in for the sake of the credit and/or remuneration? We'll talk about that aspect of a director's life in a later chapter. One of the reasons for the proliferation of independent filmmaking is that it gives the director, who is often also the screenwriter, an autonomy that is rare in the studio system and usually nonexistent for a first-time director with no track record.

In making the all important final choice you must remember that *your actors are the conduit for telling your story and conveying your throughline*. So as you watch and listen to the final reading, look at it from that perspective. Don't expect to see a finished product or a duplication of the exact image in your head, but try to make sure that the actors will be able to collaborate with you in a creative and compelling way so that together you will arrive at the creation of the characters and the fulfillment of your vision.

8

The Rehearsal Process

Now we come to what I consider to be the most fun part of the work, the period of rehearsal during which we can experiment, explore, discover, and collaborate. In the theatre it is usually a period of at least 4 weeks during which actors and director can, scene by scene and layer by layer, put together the components that will lift the text off the page and make it a living, breathing event. The film director too often either cannot or will not avail himself of this most important step in the process because of time and money concerns. But I always urge my film students to fight for at least a week or two of rehearsal no matter what the obstacles may be. There are some notable film directors who do not rehearse ahead at all. They use the period immediately before shooting each scene, often while the lighting team is doing their work. I believe the renowned Alfred Hitchcock fell into this group. There are other notable directors who insist on a minimum of 2 weeks of rehearsal time, such as Sidney Lumet and others with theatre background. I'm told that Oliver Stone took his cast to Vietnam for 6 weeks of rehearsal before shooting the celebrated war picture <u>Platoon</u>. Since I feel that this period is the one in which the director and the team can really let the creative juices flow, I can't imagine why anyone would want to be deprived of the opportunity of including it in the process.

THE TABLE READING

Although a reading of a play is a very different process from a reading of a screenplay, I like to begin the rehearsal process in much the same way for either form, with the entire team gathered around a table for the first reading. It is true that a screenplay is, for the most part, a prose rendering of what is designed primarily as a visual telling of the story. Particularly in heavily action-oriented films, the script relies in large part on description of physical action or stage directions. For both play and screenplay I advise assigning the reading of those directions to a member of the team who can do it well and who can move the reading forward. By my definition the entire team includes writer, actors, producers, designers, assistant director, stage manager, director of photography, and editor—in short anyone who will participate in the collaborative process of putting the project together. The individual participants will vary depending on whether it is a film or stage production. But it is at this point that you have the opportunity to get everyone on the same page, making the same film or realizing the same play.

INTRODUCTIONS

It is also an opportunity (and perhaps the only one, particularly in the filmmaking process) for members of the team to get to know one another, to move from the level of acquaintance to the level of collaborators, to plant the seeds of mutual trust, and to shape the often disparate members of the project into a team with a specific team ethos. Thus the first order of business is the introduction of all members to one another. It is up to the director to set the tone of this first rehearsal as a relaxed gathering of talented professionals with a common purpose. It is also up to the director at this point to convey a sense of authority tempered with humility, a sense of preparedness together with a welcoming openness. In other words, give a good performance at this point as a firm but loving and caring captain of the ship who is totally prepared and can steer a course toward success for all and you will lay the groundwork for smooth sailing with your actors and the rest of your team for the duration. First impressions are of primary importance here and insecurity is a contagious disease. No matter how nervous or uncertain you are about the choices you've made thus far, do a superb acting job and make your team feel they are in excellent hands and can trust you with their careers and their lives. *Remember that each individual comes with his/her own set of anxieties, doubts, and fears*: Will everyone like me? Am I up to the role? Does this director know what he's doing? Will my part be cut? Is the script as good as I thought it was? And those are only the anxieties related to the project at hand. Add to that mix the numerous inner dialogues such as: "I didn't sleep a wink last night; will I look puffy and awful?" "I regret that fight this morning with my lover" "I hope the babysitter knows what she's doing," etc. And at the top of the list: "Will they like my work?" The director must be aware and compassionate and help create a climate that will dissipate all these anxieties.

One sure way to help the situation is to provide good food. The standing joke is that if you want to keep actors happy, feed them. The truth is that it is not a joke; it is a necessity. Providing good food shows actors that they are being treated with respect and caring, that you are concerned enough to keep sometimes empty stomachs filled (the life of an actor can be a hard one!). Good film producers always see to it that the craft services (designated caterers) provide a generous and healthy repast. Student filmmakers often discover that craft services take up a major part of their limited budget but their wiser producers bite the bullet and see to it that the shoot is accompanied by good nourishment, even if they have to cook it themselves.

Theatre rehearsals generally start in the morning during the first 3 weeks of rehearsal, which is hard for actors who are accustomed to playing at night. They are often not morning people and are grateful for the wake-up-stay-up beverages at the food table. Therefore, at this first rehearsal coffee, tea, bagels, Danish pastry, even soft drinks, and any other tasty you can think of should be offered at the outset as a sign that your team is going to be well provided for and more good things are to come.

By the time you start rehearsals the designers have already completed the planning stage and the building of sets and costumes is underway if not completed. If possible it is most useful to have set models and/or, in the case of film, location stills as well as costume sketches at this first meeting so that everyone can see what is in store for them. (Of course in the bigger budget projects the actors have probably had fittings of their own costumes by this time, but it is useful for them to see what is being planned for others.) The aim is to bring all the elements together at the start so that individuals immediately begin to think of themselves as part of a team all working together toward a common goal.

After everyone has settled down at the table, introductions have been accomplished, snacks gathered, etc. it is advisable to say a few words to the group as a whole before the reading begins, welcoming them, and expressing your excitement about the project. I would also suggest reminding the actors that this reading is mainly for the purpose of allowing everyone to experience the script together in a relaxed fashion; everyone should feel free to express concerns or questions about the text but there is no demand for performance on their parts. The idea of this first reading of the whole script is, particularly in film, something of a luxury and in many cases is often omitted. But even if you opt to skip the reading itself, I believe the first meeting should include all of the other steps I'm outlining in the interest of creating the team effort.

DISCUSSION OF THE THROUGHLINE

After the reading of the script has been completed, we come to the next and most important phase of this meeting: the discussion of **the throughline**. Although you've no doubt discussed your throughline with some of the participants, particularly designers, director of photography (DP), location managers, etc., here lies your opportunity to communicate with your actors about your vision. *Now is the time to make sure that everyone is making the same film or creating the same realization of the play.* After sharing your throughline with the group I would ask for response or questions. If there is disagreement, uncertainty, or a lack of understanding and request for clarification, this is the time to find out. If you have done your homework well as outlined in previous chapters, your throughline should be clear and concise enough to articulate the journey that you expect to take with your team. If there are questions and/or disagreements, you must deal with them patiently, remembering that everyone wants to achieve the same goal of successful completion. You may be called upon to explain or justify your wording. If there are too many requests for explanation it might be a sign that your throughline still needs work. You must be flexible enough to allow for the possibility that your throughline needs adjustment based on the comments, questions, or concerns you are hearing. This is the most important part of the first meeting, so plan to take whatever time is necessary to reach full understanding or complete consensus. Of course, if everyone falls in line behind you immediately, either you've got an extremely compliant group or you've done your homework well!

It might be wise to take a break at this time if you haven't already done so immediately after the completion of the read through. Because after the discussion related to the throughline, I like to release everyone but the actors, and possibly the writer, in preparation for the next step in the process.

COLLABORATING WITH THE ACTORS

It is at this point that I would *begin to address the choices for the life needs of the principal characters on a one-to-one basis.* In a teaching situation or the like, discussion of the needs can be done publicly for all to hear. But in a professional situation I recommend a short private exchange with each actor. It isn't necessarily desirable to have actors concern themselves with choices for other roles, as they should be concentrating on the task of recreating the mode of human behavior for their own role.

Once again using <u>Ordinary People</u> as our prototype, let us imagine a possible dialogue between director and the actor playing Conrad:

DIRECTOR: *Tim, I think Conrad's life need—in terms of my throughline for the film—is to get rid of guilt. What do you think?*

TIM: *Well, I was thinking more along the lines of his need to get his mother's love. She seems to have constantly rejected him in favor of his big brother and now she's shutting him out.*

DIRECTOR: *I have no doubt that he wants and needs his mother's love. But if that were the* **priority** *need for the context of the script, wouldn't he be making more of an effort to please her? And would he let her go at the end without running after her and trying to persuade her to stay? He does reach out to her on occasion from scene to scene, but he also seems to be more provocative and accusative overall than one whose priority is to get love.*

TIM: *Well, I'm afraid that the need to get rid of guilt might make him much less sympathetic. People lash out when they're feeling guilty—or withdraw completely.*

DIRECTOR: *That's true, but we can counteract that with a careful choice of scene needs and actions as we explore the moment-to-moment behavior.*

At this point the actor might agree to try your choice or continue to argue the virtues of his. If the latter is the case, I would not belabor it. I would suggest to the actor that it might be useful to try it both ways and see what works. You must be constantly aware that the actor is thinking only about his role and the task that lies ahead for him, whereas you are thinking about your throughline and the whole. But rather than assume a dictatorial stance or get into a protracted debate at this point, I believe *it is always more desirable to give the actor a chance to try out his ideas even if they disagree with yours.* You can always alter or adjust as you go forward. And you never know—you might discover that the actor's choice has merit and might possibly be a better choice than yours. A word of caution here regarding a trap that I often see my students fall into: *Don't try to personalize your own connection to the choice and then attempt to transfer that choice to the actor.* Remember, you are using the actor's brain/computer, not satisfying your own. Although you've done considerable homework and think you know what you want, it is essential to stay flexible and leave yourself open to what you might derive from the creativity of others.

There is also the possibility that the actor to whom you've just communicated your life need choice will stare at you blankly and say something like "I don't know what that means" or "I don't work that way." Don't panic. The actor is simply suggesting that he uses a different vocabulary based on his training or that he relies more on moment-to-moment inspiration and doesn't practice a particular craft. (Presumably you have this knowledge of the actor prior to rehearsal if you've followed my suggestions about the casting process.) If this is the case, note the following points: First, you can try substitute wording such as "your overall objective in the script," or "your end goal," or "the drive or want that influences all your behavior in the larger sense." Second, since you've already stated your choice and the actor has heard it, it has been placed in the computer/brain of the actor and you might see its effect anyway. This is because, as I've said, most actors are sponges who soak up everything they hear. This can be an asset in this situation, although at times if you've chosen your words unwisely it can be a big liability. In any case, you have accomplished a kind of communication, however subliminal, of what you have in mind for the development of the character and you have given the actor a sense of how you hope the character will develop.

There are many apocryphal stories about the antagonisms and sometimes outright hostilities that can develop in the actor–director relationship. I grew up with one about an actress who supposedly challenged the aforementioned Mr. Hitchcock during a shoot. When asked to walk from one end of the room to the other she asked:

"But why would I do that? What's my motivation?"
"To get your check, madam!" snapped Mr. Hitchcock

Seriously, I feel that many of these negative anecdotes stem from a refusal on the part of the director to understand the actor's craft and language and to clearly communicate in a manner that conveys intent to collaborate rather than dictate.

It is of course entirely dependent on your time schedule, but in my opinion the introduction, reading of the script, discussion of the throughline, and one-on-one dialogue with the actors about life needs are quite enough to tackle for the first day. *It is always useful to allow the actors time to privately process whatever they've experienced and learned at each meeting or rehearsal.* It gives them an opportunity to integrate or reject a choice, or return with questions. Although that is most desirable, if time is really short, I would suggest tightening and condensing so that you can put all of the above into the morning session, after which you can break for lunch and have the actors return in the afternoon for the start of the scene-by-scene rehearsal.

SCENE-BY-SCENE REHEARSAL

The order in which you choose to rehearse scene by scene might vary depending on whether the project is a screenplay or a play. Usually in the theatre one wants to start at the beginning and work scene by scene until the end is reached. It is said that Mike Nichols often rehearses even his film projects in sequence. As films are usually shot out of sequence to accommodate schedules, location, technical demands, and so on, each scene can often be rehearsed out of sequence. For example, Judd Hirsch was probably called in for a period of time to rehearse all the Conrad/Psychiatrist scenes together. And they were probably all shot out of sequence within the same couple of weeks. Sometimes a director might choose to address the more challenging or difficult scenes first, particularly if there is a time limitation.

But the rehearsal process is, in terms of my approach, much the same for both theatre and film. The major difference, as I've said, is time. Rehearsing a play usually allows us 3 weeks of 8-hour days in which to gradually, layer by layer, arrive at the final choices. This is followed by a few 12-hour days in which to get all the technical demands straightened out and integrated. Next there are dress rehearsals, which are much like performances and previews, which are performances followed by directors' notes. In film, everything in this phase of the work must be tightened and condensed. Thus there is considerable reliance on the talent, technique, and persona of the actors to fill in the gaps.

Proper scheduling of rehearsals is hugely important. The thing that is most difficult for actors is the waiting. Hours of hanging around without fruitful work can really destroy the creative process. It is most important to confer with your stage manager or assistant director and arrange individual schedules for the actors so that they have a minimum of wasted idle time at the rehearsal hall. This means that you have to develop a strong sense of what can be accomplished on a particular scene in a given amount of time. (Once again, I bless the television training ground regarding the use of time.)

No matter what scene you start with, the process is the same. Still seated at a table together, **first review the throughline** with the actors. Then have the actors read the scene in its entirety. Next **reexamine the chosen life needs** of the characters. Are the actors comfortable with the choices? Have they come up with another idea in the interim between the last meeting and the present? If so, suggest reading the scene again with the alternate life need choice in mind. As I've suggested, you may be in for a pleasant surprise. But if you still think your choice is the most useful one, there are many ways to steer an intransigent actor away from the undesirable choice. With male actors I've used the line: "Well, it's interesting, but it makes you seem weak." Few men want to hear that! With female actors you might try something like: "It's a possibility, but it makes you less attractive." In other words, don your psychologist hat and gently but firmly lead them away from their choice and toward yours—if you are really convinced that yours is the better one.

Once the life need is firmly in place, the next discussion should be about the choice of **scene need** for that particular scene. *Remember, the scene need is pursued **in order to** pursue the life need, so the life need must be agreed upon before you can proceed.* Here again I would offer your choice and see what the response is to it. If there is resistance you may be called upon to support the logic or the usefulness of your choice. Whenever you make a suggestion of needs or offer a direction *it is critically important that you watch your actor's eyes.* The eyes will tell you volumes when the actor is unwilling to reveal verbally what is really going on inside that computer/brain. A blank or glazed look usually means resistance or lack of comprehension. A few blinks can mean an effort to process what has just been heard. A gleam or slight widening of the eye can mean discovery of something useful. An involuntary up and down nod of the head means you've hit pay dirt. Another read through is advisable after the scene needs have been selected. Now the actors have the blueprint or **outline** with which to begin the work.

With a play script and the luxury of time that the theatre rehearsals afford, you might want to have a more in-depth discussion at this point about the back story: history of the character before the play or screenplay takes place, such as where did he/she go to school, how much education was there? Is she a virgin? Is he? How many women has he slept with before he met her? Was she abused by her father as a child? In other words, elements of the character's background that are either subtly suggested or not covered at all in the script but which will influence the recreation of the behavior of the character. Sometimes the writer will have to be sought out for answers to these questions, but often the director and actor, in the absence of the writer, must collaborate on the creation of the back story. Some directors actually present their actors with written biographies of their characters. To save grief later on in the process it is important that both parties start out with agreement about the back story.

Of course these discussions must also take place between actor and director in the process of bringing a film script to life. But in the interests of time it is often necessary to have them during coffee breaks, at lunch, or in the actor's trailer during lighting waits or whenever you can grab an actor outside of the actual rehearsal/shooting schedule. Since the actor's process is one of gradual layering, it is important to make the actor feel that you are always available to answer questions. Whatever answers you offer are sure to reside in the actor's subtext eventually, giving the character the depth and dimension that make us believe we are seeing something real.

An example of this might be—going back to our prototype Ordinary People—the moment when Conrad's Grandmother is alone in the kitchen with Mother, who has just told her that her son is seeing a psychiatrist. The line is brief but potentially loaded.

"A Jewish doctor?" she asks. The subtextual question would be whether the grandmother is anti-Semitic or just curious. The anti-Semitic choice would certainly give the line a specific spin. As there is possibly a smaller Jewish population in Lake Forest, I leave it to you as to what you think Meg Mundy, the actor who played the Grandmother, and Robert Redford decided on as a choice (for a clue, look at our throughline for the film).

MOVEMENT IN THE SCENE AND THE USE OF PROPS

Assuming that both you and your actors are comfortable and reasonably secure with your choices of needs, it is now time to get the actors up on their feet. *Beware of too much time spent sitting around a table.* Some actors like to stall and postpone the inevitable, particularly the less secure entry-level actors with whom film students often work, and find more and more things to talk about. Now it is time to insist sweetly but firmly that they get up on their feet.

Students always ask me when and how I advise *blocking* a scene, i.e., directing the physical movement or *staging* as it is often called in the theatre. The truth is that unless there is a very specific demand to satisfy either sight lines (theatre) or camera position and special effects demands (film), and in view of the fact that *we want the physical movement to be arrived at organically by the actors in pursuit of their needs and actions,* I don't even advise thinking of the physical movement as blocking, at least certainly not at this stage. Some directors seem to be under the misapprehension that their entire task in directing actors involves telling the actors where and when to sit, stand, enter, leave, etc. as per their preconceived storyboards or ideas, as well as how to utter a line in terms of speed and or volume to get a certain dynamic in a given scene. I cannot subscribe to this external and basically mechanical approach to the work. It seems to me to negate the whole idea of collaboration, turning the actors into something like robots and robbing the whole process of creativity and discovery. Although storyboarding is altogether necessary in the film director's preparation, I prefer that you wait until after a scene is rehearsed with actors to complete that task, even if it means working late into each night.

Before the actors can begin to move, however, they must have a clear idea of the geography of a given scene. The first order of business in this next stage of the work is to give the actors all the specific information they need about the location of the scene: doors, windows, placement of furniture, kind of furniture, props that might be present, etc. As for the use of hand props (books, magazines, a bowl, an *objet d'art*, kitchen implements, etc.), I advise introducing them as soon as possible or, at the very least, informing the actors as to what will be present for their use. Although it is difficult for the actors to handle props as they are struggling to deal with unfamiliar dialogue while holding scripts, I've found that the presence of or even just the awareness of the possibility of props often stimulates creativity and produces ideas for the behavior that accompanies pursuing actions through objects (i.e., caressing a lover's sweater in the lover's absence). Often in the course of rehearsal an actor will get an idea and request a specific prop that might not have been indicated in the script. It is usually a good idea to trust your actors' instincts and let them experiment with the ideas that might be suggested (assuming of course that you've chosen good actors!). Since it is the actor who is attempting to make what is on the page become a flesh and blood human being, it is advisable to give the actor every aid and as much leeway as possible.

And then there is the lucky accident. Something happens unexpectedly in a rehearsal or a take that wasn't planned. The accident is sometimes pure gold, helping to deepen the scene, or get the laugh, or fill in a visual gap. An apocryphal story about this kind of lucky accident is told about a scene between Marlon Brando and Eva Marie Saint in <u>On the Waterfront</u>. (Once again if you haven't seen this film, run to the nearest DVD or VHS rental store as it is an American classic.) It is a scene in which they are walking away from a disturbing meeting in the church. It seems cold and gray but there is a sexual tension that provides the heat between the two characters as they are getting to know one another. As the story goes, during a take Eva Marie accidentally dropped one of her gloves as she was putting them on. Marlon picked up the glove and, acting out of the instinct of the moment, studied it for a second and then attempted to put his hand inside it. Elia Kazan, brilliant director that he was, knew enough to keep the cameras rolling and printed the take. In his review, Roger Ebert, the well-known film critic, singled out this moment as having given the scene added "texture." Actually, that small accident gave us a clear visual snapshot of the character's subtextual need at that moment. Trust your actors and they may find you gold!

STARTING THE SCENE

Once having acclimated your actors to their environment and what it might contain, the big question is how to begin the scene. Where will the actors be placed and, even more importantly, what will they be doing? Understand that when I refer to "doing" I mean the moment-to-moment psychological action verbs, not the activity (physical action). The action verb, which lies in the subtext for the actor, motivating and influencing the behavior, can often affect the activity. Remember, the activity is something like sleeping, walking, knitting, combing one's hair, etc. The activity of combing one's hair, for example, might be pursued with any number of action choices, such as **to caress** or **to attack**, and each choice will give the activity a different rhythm. I like to *choose the action first and then find an appropriate activity through which to pursue it*. Since you don't want one actor waiting for the other actor to start so that he/she can react, it is useful to suggest a beginning action to each actor at the start of the scene. Then they can immediately both start the give and take motivated by their sets of needs.

THE JUMP BALL

Using the game of basketball as a model of how to make a beginning, I like to call these first action choices *the jump ball*. In that game the play is begun as the referee throws the ball into the air and one designated player from each opposing team goes after it. The player that gets it or bats it toward a teammate puts the ball in play and it is then moved down the court toward the basket. If you begin the scene with this jump ball the needs are pursued from the top, just as in life, and no one is caught waiting. This is particularly desirable in theatre. In film we have the ability to choose a shot or cut around what we don't want in the editing process. However, working this way will not only help the actors, but also give the director a much broader palette of options in the edit.

The choice of the jump ball action is key and if selected properly can help each actor find the moment-to-moment behavior that follows. It is advisable therefore to choose an action that is derived from the needs rather than from the lines in the text. For example, suppose the scene is about two lovers who are about to have a quarrel. The woman is ironing a shirt (activity) with the action **to accuse.** The direction would be, in this instance, *accuse the shirt* because, let us say, in the previous scene she has learned that her lover has been unfaithful and it is his shirt she is ironing. This will affect both the rhythm and the manner in which she irons. The lover enters the room with the line "What are you doing?" The activity is entering the room. The action could be chosen for the line, i.e., a simple **to question**, which would be obvious and therefore quite a dull choice. It could be more confrontational, as in **to challenge**, or if the lover senses her suspicion, perhaps **to apologize**. How does one make the choice? The choice comes from the needs. What if the woman's life need is **to get love** and her scene need is **to prove herself as a woman**? Then the choice **to accuse** might be useful. The actor would be accusing in order to prove herself as a woman in order to get love. But if her life need was **to get love** and her scene need was **to hold on to her self-respect**, then her jump ball action might be more self-protective as in **to withdraw** into the ironing.

By the same token, if the man's life need were **to prove his manhood** and his scene need were **to free himself**, then the choice of **to challenge** as his jump ball action might be a useful one. However, if his scene need were **to get rid of guilt** with that life need then his first action might well be **to apologize**. So you see, a simple opening line can be invested with all kinds of meaning or motivate many forms of behavior depending on the choice of action. The goal is to put the ball into play or, in our terms, start the moment-to-moment interaction.

THE MOMENT TO MOMENT

Once the moment-to-moment give and take between actors has begun my advice is to let the actors find their way, making notes in your script when you see them intuitively arriving at action choices you want to see again. *Remember that the actors are working in the moment and might not even remember what they did.* If they come up with something you really like and you want to keep it in, you must identify it for them by saying "I really liked it when you charmed her on that line about the ironing," or words to that effect. Be as specific as possible. *Put it into the actor's conscious level*, i.e., the computer/brain, or you may never see that particular choice again.

Many beginning directors, upon discovering the usefulness of these little action words, go through all the dialogue in their preparation work and assign an action to practically every line. When they begin rehearsal with the actors they already have preconceived notions of what the actions should be and they immediately begin assigning these choices. This is folly in my opinion, as it completely eliminates the creativity of the actor and negates the collaborative process, in addition to robbing the director of the possibility of allowing the actors to discover truly organic moment-to-moment behavior. Start them off with the strong and appropriate jump ball and see where that takes them.

COMMUNICATING WITH THE ACTORS

It is useful to develop your own shorthand or speed writing technique as you will find that at times the actors' choices of actions will be so intuitive and/or reflexive that they will go by very quickly. So as not to have to interrupt the moment it is important that you be able to (1) quickly identify the action being pursued and (2) jot it down in the margin of your script next to the line or lines where it appeared. Then when you've stopped the actors, perhaps at the end of a beat, you can discuss with the actors more specifically what they've arrived at and decide what works well and what should be changed. (Note: See Appendix A for exercises to sharpen the director's ability to make quick action identification.)

In talking to actors I try to state things positively and avoid negatives such as "don't do that" or "I don't like that." I prefer to say "instead of ——, why don't you try ——." Actors are subjected to enormous doses of rejection and are, by definition, asked to expose their very innards in the course of the work. This makes them extremely vulnerable human beings. The slightest negative can often be mistaken as disparaging or a slur. "She doesn't like me" or "He thinks I can't act" may be what the actor is internalizing. So it is important to remain acutely aware of the actors' delicate psyche, however engrossed you may become in making the work perfect. The most important element in the relationship between actor and director is **mutual trust**. Without that the process can become painful indeed. You must trust the actor's instinct, intelligence, and craft. If the actor feels respected and cared for and is assured that the director is prepared and watching every detail as a contributing third eye, trust will follow.

I recall my actor father who, while rehearsing for a Broadway play, came home one night agonizing over the fact that the director had given the cast copious notes after a run-through but had no notes for him. Was it possible that the director thought what he was doing was hopeless? I suggested that he confront the director the next day and ask him why he had omitted him in the notes session. To my surprise Dad followed my advice and related to me that night what the director had replied to his query: "But Roger, what you're doing is perfect! I had nothing to add to it." That director would have spared my father a nervous night had he thought to share his delight with his actor. Actors need stroking and reassuring. Let them know when they're doing something you don't want to see again, but also let them know when they are doing something you like, as often as possible.

Another common error I see some of my students make in the rehearsal process seems to stem from a fear of interrupting the actors as they work. Suddenly the director forgets his role and becomes audience, politely allowing the actors to keep going, even though they are taking the character in the wrong direction or making choices the director doesn't really want. What ensues is then more like a run-through and is counterproductive to the concept of rehearsal. If the actors are allowed to go to the end of a scene, there is no way they will remember most of what they have discovered along the way. *Run-throughs should take place after all the beats have been put together and everyone knows what the choices are.* They don't belong at the beginning of the rehearsal process. If you allow the actors to run from start to finish, certain choices will lodge themselves in the actor's brain and remain there. If you want to make changes it then becomes more difficult for the actor to replace what has already been chosen so you are not really doing the actors any favors in allowing them to continue. Although it is difficult and sometimes irritating, actors understand that they have to be stopped in order to find out what is working and to discard what is not.

Perhaps you are wondering how to delineate **a beat** or when it is appropriate to stop and make a suggestion or offer a direction. A beat in my parlance is a segment of a scene that is much like a phrase in music. *The beat ends when the subject matter changes, there is an entrance or an exit, or the scene takes another direction.* For example, once again using <u>Ordinary People</u> to illustrate, think of the first scene between Conrad and the psychiatrist. The first beat is the entrance of the boy and the doctor's attempt to seat him and help him feel at ease. Once he is seated the beat changes and the questioning begins. The second beat ends when Conrad begins to resist and reveals his conflict, etc. It is up to the director to delineate the beats for himself so that he can work a piece at a time. What I like to do is rehearse a beat then stop and discuss and/or identify the choices or suggest changes. Then go back from the top and try the beat again. When I am satisfied that the beat is going well (and is moving in the direction that serves the throughline), I will suggest starting from the top of the beat and moving on to the next beat. But I'd rather not move on to the next beat until I feel that the actors are secure with the shape of the beat at hand.

It may be my early training as a pianist that introduced me to this way of working. I was instructed to work on a phrase until I'd mastered it and then repeat it and move on to the next phrase. I'll tell you one thing: I certainly learned the piece and had it committed to memory by the time I finished—and the actors, by the time they are finished working this way, often know all their lines and are spared the agony of memorizing them at home!

Remember this above all: *Do not take your eyes off your actors.* Often I see a director sitting at rehearsal with eyes glued to the script as though he/she is the prompter and I wonder how on earth that director can possibly know what the actors are doing. By the time you've reached the rehearsal stage, you should be familiar enough with the text so as not to have to stare at it. Because both on camera and on stage the smallest move or movement is noticed and absorbed by the audience, it is essential that you pay attention to every detail the actors might introduce. A simple shrug or flick of the ash of a cigarette might not be on the printed page but might speak volumes in the moment. Particularly in film, where the camera can act as a magnifying glass, the slightest wink of an eye can be telling. A move of an actor on stage can distract, upstage other actors, or underline an idea. Have faith that the work on the text has already been done. Now it is time to give your full attention to lifting the words off the page and breathing life into them. Therefore, with the exception of referring to the text quickly to make your notes about action choices, your eyes must be on your actors. In the later stages of a play rehearsal if the actors are still struggling with remembering lines while off-book, have your stage manager hold the script and cue them. Film actors have an advantage when it comes to learning lines. Film scenes are usually much shorter than play scenes. They are not only easier to learn but there is also the safety net of another take if an actor should mess up.

A SAMPLE SCENE

Let us take a sample scene with which to explore the beginning steps of the rehearsal process. Assuming that by now you are surely familiar with <u>Death of a Salesman</u> by Arthur Miller in its totality, let us use the early scene between Biff and Happy, the two brothers, as a model for our investigation. Here is how it starts in the Penguin paperback copy (ISBN 0-14-048-134-6) of the text published in 1976:

> *Light has risen on the boys' room. Unseen, Willy is heard talking to himself. Biff gets out of bed, comes downstage a bit, and stands attentively. Biff is two years older than his brother Happy, well built, but in these days bears a worn air and seems less self-assured. He has succeeded less and his dreams are stronger and less acceptable than Happy's. Happy is tall, powerfully made. Sexuality is like a visible color on him, or a scent that many women have discovered. He, like his brother, is lost, but in a different way, for he has never allowed himself to turn his face toward defeat and is thus more confused and hard-skinned, although seemingly more content.*

HAPPY (*getting out of bed*): He's going to get his license taken away if he keeps that up. I'm getting nervous about him, y'know Biff?

BIFF: His eyes are going.

HAPPY: No, I've driven with him. He sees all right. He just doesn't keep his mind on it. I drove into the city with him last week. He stops at a green light and then it turns red and he goes. (*He laughs.*)

BIFF: Maybe he's color-blind.

HAPPY: Pop? Why he's got the finest eye for color in the business. You know that.

BIFF (*sitting down on his bed*): I'm going to sleep.

HAPPY: You're not still sour on Dad, are you Biff?

BIFF: He's all right I guess.

WILLY (*in the living room*): Yes sir, eighty thousand miles—eighty-two thousand!

BIFF: You smoking?

HAPPY (*holding out a pack of cigarettes*): Want one?

BIFF (*taking a cigarette*): I can never sleep when I smell it.

WILLY: What a simonizing job, heh!

HAPPY (*with deep sentiment*): Funny Biff y'know? Us sleeping in here again? The old beds. (*He pats his bed affectionately.*) All the talk that went across those two beds huh? Our whole lives.

BIFF: Yeah. Lotta dreams and plans.

HAPPY (*with a deep masculine laugh*): About five hundred women would like to know what was said in this room.

(*They share a soft laugh*)

BIFF: Remember that big Betsy something—what the hell was her name—over on Bushwick Avenue?

HAPPY (*combing his hair*): With the collie dog!

BIFF: That's the one. I got you in there, remember?

HAPPY: Yeah, that was my first time—I think. Boy, there was a pig! (*They laugh almost crudely.*) You taught me everything I know about women. Don't forget that.

BIFF: I bet you forgot how bashful you used to be. Especially with girls.

HAPPY: Oh I still am, Biff.

BIFF: Oh, go on.

HAPPY: I just control it, that's all. I think I got less bashful and you got more so. What happened Biff? Where's the old humor, the old confidence? (*He shakes Biff's knee. Biff gets up and moves restlessly about the room.*) What's the matter?

BIFF: Why does Dad mock me all the time?

HAPPY: He's not mocking you, he—-

BIFF: Everything I say there's a twist of mockery on his face. I can't get near him.

HAPPY: He just wants you to make good, that's all. I wanted to talk to you about Dad for a long time, Biff. Something's—happening to him. He—talks to himself.

BIFF: I noticed that this morning. But he always mumbled.

HAPPY: But not so noticeable. It got so embarrassing I sent him to Florida. And you know something? Most of the time he's talking to you.

BIFF: What's he say about me?

HAPPY: I can't make it out.

BIFF: What's he say about me?

HAPPY: I think the fact that you're not settled, that you're still kind of up in the air . . .

BIFF: There's one or two other things depressing him, Happy.
HAPPY: What do you mean?
BIFF: Never mind. Just don't lay it all on me.
HAPPY: But I think if you just got started—I mean—is there any
future for you out there?
BIFF: I tell ya, Hap, I don't know what the future is. I don't know—
what I'm supposed to want.

Since this last is the beginning of a new beat, we'll stop here.
But bear with me for a moment, for with the purpose of making a
point, I'm going to show you the same scene as it appears in the
Dramatists Play Service printing which is called the "authorized
acting edition" and must have been published sometime after the
Broadway production in 1949:

> (*Willy starts out of the bedroom, goes to the kitchen—talking to himself.*
> *Biff comes downstage a bit and stands attentively. He is two years older*
> *than his brother Happy, well-built but in these days bears a worn air, and*
> *seems less self assured. He has succeeded less, and his dreams are stronger*
> *and less acceptable than Happy's. Happy is tall, powerfully made.*
> *Sexuality is like a visible color on him, or a scent that many women have*
> *discovered. He, like his brother, is lost, but in a different way, for he has*
> *never allowed himself to turn his face toward defeat and is thus more con-*
> *fused and hardskinned, although seemingly happier. Both Biff and Happy*
> *are underdressed*)

HAPPY: He's going to get his license taken away if he keeps that
up. I'm getting nervous about him, y'know Biff?
BIFF: His eyes are going.
HARRY: No I've driven with him. He sees all right. He just doesn't
keep his mind on it. I drove into the city with him last week. He
stops at a green light and then it turns red and he goes. (*Laughs*)
BIFF: Maybe he's color-blind!
HARRY: Pop? Why he's got the finest eye for color in the business.
You know that.
BIFF: I'm going to sleep. (*Fixes bed*)
HAPPY: You're not still sour on Dad are you Biff?
BIFF: He's all right, I guess. (*Starts UP*)
WILLY (*pacing in the kitchen. Unfastens collar and tie. Biff stops, listens*):
Yes, sir. Eighty thousand miles . . . eighty-two thousand!
BIFF: You smoking?

HAPPY: Want one? (*Offers BIFF his lighted cigarette.*)

BIFF (*taking it, crossing R., sits chair*): I can never sleep when I smell it.

WILLY (*in kitchen*): What a simonizing job, heh! (*Exits out kitchen door L.*)

HAPPY (*with deep sentiment*): Funny, Biff, y'know?—us sleeping in here again? The old beds. All the talk that went across those two beds, huh? Our whole lives.

BIFF: Yeah . . . lotta dreams and plans.

HAPPY (*with a laugh, deep and masculine*): About five hundred women would like to know what was said in this room! (*They share a soft laugh.*)

BIFF: Remember that big Betsy something—what the hell was her name, over on Bushwick Avenue?

HAPPY: With the collie dog!

BIFF: That's the one. I got you in there remember? (*Both laugh.*)

HAPPY: Yeah, that was my first time—(*Crosses U.L., turns*) I think. (*Combs hair*) Boy, there was a pig! (*They laugh, almost crudely. Linda takes Willy's coat, exits from bedroom.*) You taught me everything I know about women. Don't forget that.

BIFF: I bet you forgot how bashful you used to be. Especially with girls.

HAPPY: Oh I still am, Biff . . .

BIFF: Oh, go on!

HAPPY (*crossing D. to L. of Biff*): I just control it, that's all. I think I got less bashful and you got more so. What happened, Biff? (*Sits, above Biff , puts arm around him.*) Where's the old humor? The old confidence? (*Biff rises, crosses L. to above chest, puts cigarette out in small can on floor above chest.*) What's the matter?

And so on. . . . Now let's look at the differences between the two versions. The dialogue may be exactly the same, and what I am about to point out may seem like nit-picking, but these subtle differences can make specific changes in how the actor perceives the character, how the actor approaches the line or the direction of the scene or even the role itself. For example:

1. The acting version, guided by director Elia Kazan's choices and no doubt suggested by his throughline, describes Happy as "seemingly happier" than Biff, whereas the Penguin version uses the words "seemingly more content." Again, this may seem like a small detail,

but it is my contention that the computer/brain of the actor will respond differently to each of those two words.

2. In the acting version, Biff and Happy are "underdressed," which I assume to mean in their underwear. No such reference is made in the Penguin. Observation will show you that people behave very differently depending on how much or how little they are wearing. The nature of behavior is definitely affected by the manner and amount of dress.

3. The line "maybe he's color-blind" is followed by an exclamation point in the acting version. There is no exclamation point in the Penguin. That little detail might suggest to the actor that the action on that line might be **to discover** as the exclamation point gives the line more weight. The line by itself with no punctuation could be **to shrug off** or **to toss off** or anything else for that matter.

4. On Biff's line "I'm going to sleep" the stage direction in the acting version is "fixes bed." In the Penguin version Biff is "sitting on his bed." Perhaps the latter choice would make him appear to be simply considering the move and more hesitant, less decisive?

5. In the cigarette beat, the Penguin version has Happy holding out a pack of cigarettes with "want one?" In the acting version, Happy offers Biff his own lighted cigarette—a much more intimate gesture.

6. In the Penguin, with the lines "What happened Biff? Where's the old humor, the old confidence?" Happy shakes Biff's knee. The action choice might be **to incite**. In the acting version, Kazan has Happy putting his arm around his brother; the action choice might well be **to comfort**.

One might deduce from the differences in the acting version that Kazan was interested in reestablishing the relationship between the two brothers after a long separation.

Why, you may ask, am I bothering to point out these tiny details and what point am I trying to make? Well it is simply this: At the risk of offending and even possibly angering those of you who are also writers, I must tell you that my advice is to *delete everything in the script that is in italics or parentheses,* purports to give you the emotional state of the character, or dictates the movement of the actors, with the exception of the critical plot moves of course, such as "He leaves" or "she throws the keys out the window."

Certainly with remakes of already produced screenplays or revivals of plays, you are likely to find that the script with which you are working includes, however subtly, the concept of the original director. You must start with a fresh concept—your own—not be persuaded to replicate someone else's vision. But when you are working with a new original script you may find that the writer has included everything that occurred to him/her as he/she mentally visualized the line reading or the action as it was being written. And thus that writer is attempting, consciously or subconsciously, to direct the director with instructions like "laughingly" or "he scratches his nose." On occasion, these writer instructions may be helpful, if for no other purpose than to allow us to peek inside the writer's head as he/she wrote. But often they are counterproductive and interfere with the design for the throughline or the actor's creative process. The writer's perspective is very different from the director's and the actor's. Each of the three elements must be allowed its contribution. It is the successful blending of the perspectives of all three disciplines that results in a cohesive and clear result.

I'll let you in on a little secret. Actors in training are often instructed by their teachers to cross out everything in parentheses in their scripts so as to eliminate distraction and clogging of the computer/brain with extraneous ideas. So we as directors, after absorbing everything the writer has tried to tell us and factoring the information into the structuring of the throughline and the outline of the characters, might want to eliminate the distractions and give the actors clean scripts.

It is useful, I think, to review one's throughline before the start of each rehearsal. Since we are simply exploring the process, for the sake of expedience let us use one of the throughlines we mentioned previously for purposes of beginning the work (although after this I urge you to come up with your own throughline for the material and try following the steps for it as a continuation of the exercise).

> *"The small individual businessman, in his desperate attempt to survive the growing quest for material wealth and need to fulfill the myth of the American Dream, is dooming himself to eventual eradication."*

If you remember, we decided that Willy Loman was the protagonist with this particular throughline. We also said that Biff seemed to be swinging back and forth between the opposing antagonist and protagonist sides in his search for where he belonged and that Happy seemed to fall in the middle or mediator position. In terms of the journey implied by the throughline, it would seem that this scene that we are working on, coming as early as it does in the structure of the script, ought to be about the struggle of these two sons to find their places within the myth. Should they follow their father's path or strike out on their own toward new horizons? Where are the answers? Can they find them within each other? As the brothers have been separated for a while, before they can address the main issue they must reestablish the relationship. Toward that end, they've just gone out on a double date together that Happy set up. Was it a successful evening? Fun or strained? Questions such as these must be part of the director's investigation before meeting with the actors so that the director is prepared for the actors' questions.

DESIGNING THE ARC

Of course, before this exploration of the text in terms of the characters, it is assumed that the director has examined the position of the scene and its place in the overall arc of the script. *I like to think of each scene as a station on the journey.* The director must first have decided on the design of the arc:

Where is the top of the arc, or the moment of climax?
How is the build toward that moment or event going to be constructed?
What are the obstacles to the climb?
Where does the particular scene on which you are working lie in relation to the top of the arc?
What is the design of the smaller arc in the scene itself?
What are the obstacles in the scene?
What is the moment of greatest risk or discovery or change?

Here is where the director's choice rules. Let me remind you that each actor is concerned only with the development of his/her own character and cannot think in terms of the overall design. That is the director's job. So in guiding the actors in both the needs and the action choices, the director must factor in the design of the scene and the necessity of creating the interaction and/or tensions that will create the arc. With all this in mind, the next order of business is making the choice of scene needs. Be ready with the choices, having thought it through in your homework, even though you will need to collaborate with the actor in making the final selection.

CHOOSING NEEDS

Let us, for the sake of this example, review what we discussed as possible Life Needs for these characters in a previous chapter, based on the throughline given earlier. For Biff it was **to find his identity** and for Happy it was **to get love**. Biff seems to be roiling and broiling in the scene—restless, questioning, concerned with what his father thinks of him, etc. If you remember I pointed out that **to free himself** (from his father) might be an alternative choice for a Life Need but if we choose **find his identity** as his priority need, why not put the need **to free himself** (from his father) in the scene as a first step in his search. Again, I must remind you that *these needs are not something that the character knows about himself*. They are in the subtext of the character and the consciousness of the actor and will inform the general behavior of the character as well as the specific action choices on a moment-to-moment basis.

With the Life Need **to get love**, Happy's path seems clear. He is the constant moderator. Like most siblings, he probably has had a love/hate relationship with his brother. But at present he seems to need an ally to help save the family's equilibrium, and he seems to want to restore a relationship that frayed with absence. Therefore, let us choose the Scene Need to win Biff. Now let us look at what we've set up:

BIFF: **To free himself (from his father) in order to find his identity**
HAPPY: **To win Biff in order to get love**

Note that I put "from his father" in parentheses. That is because the use of those words depends entirely on the actor's connection to them. If the actor playing Biff actually loves his father deeply he would need to substitute someone else from his own life who made him feel trapped in a relationship in order to personalize the need.

Have we made choices that will create a tension or stress between the two men and help build the arc of the scene? (When I use the word *arc* I am referring to the shape of the aforementioned mountain climb. We need to structure a little arc in each scene as well as the larger arc of the whole play or screenplay.) On the face of it, it would certainly seem that the characters would move in opposition in pursuing their needs; one wants to get out of a situation and the other wants to keep him at his side. But also remember that *everything we do in our own homework stage must be written in pencil so that when we try it with the actors we can remain flexible until we are sure that the choices are useful for the actors.*

What point might we designate as the top of the arc in the scene? Again, for the sake of this exercise, let us say that we are building to the following high moment of the scene. It is reached after several beats in which each brother has opened up and shared his thoughts to the other:

BIFF: I'm tellin' you kid, if you were with me I'd be happy out there.
HAPPY: See Biff, everybody around me is so false that I'm constantly lowering my ideals . . .
BIFF: Baby, together we'd stand up for one another, we'd have someone to trust.
HAPPY: But if I were around you . . .
BIFF: Hap, the trouble is we weren't brought up to grub for money. I don't know how to do it . . .
HAPPY (*shouts*): Neither can I!
BIFF (*shouts*): Then let's go!

This is the point at which they seem to come together supposedly to beat the game and attain the myth so the scene requires that we design the gradual warming up of the relationship, sharing and finding common ground that will enable them to get to this point. This awareness will help guide us in our beginning choices, as we now know how long it will take to get from the beginning of the climb to the top of the arc. We certainly don't want to start halfway up and get them there too soon, and this knowledge will inform us as to the possible jump ball choices.

It has been proven to me time and time again that *the beginning of the scene is the place that demands most attention.* If you get the scene started properly in the right direction with the actors organically connected to the needs, the actors will, in all probability, be able to do most of the work on the remainder of the scene for you. If the team gets the beginning right, the rest of the work may well fall into place with the help of the actors' imagination and moment-to-moment pursuit of their needs.

Let us say that the boys' old room is upstairs with a window directly over the kitchen window (enabling Biff and Happy to overhear Willy's mutterings). There would have to be twin beds, separated by a nightstand, which holds a lamp and an ashtray. There also might be a bookcase or shelf arrangement that could house athletic trophies and perhaps a football, basketball, or soft-ball—or perhaps all three to help bring their past together into the present. We might also want a dresser or chest with a mirror, which would give the actors other opportunities for action choices and activities. A decision would have to be made as to their stage of undress, as they are preparing to go to bed. But the jump ball can help us with this, so sometimes it is useful to start with that choice.

Again, I most often find that the best way to make that initial choice of action is from the scene need, not necessarily from the dialogue or lack of it. For example, in this scene, Biff is silent at the top and Happy initiates the dialogue with "He's going to get his license taken away . . ." Biff's scene need is **to free himself** so perhaps we might start him at the window, gazing out at the backyard, with the action choice **to withdraw from Happy**—an internalized, self-investigatory choice. Happy's need is **to win him**. If we want to start with an action derived from the scene need we might choose **to impress** Biff. This would require an accompanying activity. Perhaps he is doing some preretiring push-ups and impressing Biff with his stamina. So the character *outlines* for the jump ball would look like this:

BIFF: **To withdraw in order to free himself (from Dad) in order find his identity**.
HAPPY: **To impress Biff in order to win him in order to get love**

And the opening might look something like this:

BIFF stands at the window, gazing out. (Action to withdraw as a means of shutting out Happy and his father.) HAPPY is noisily doing push-ups to attract his attention.
HAPPY (action to impress): He's going to get his license taken away if he keeps that up. (No response from Biff. This might motivate a change in action choice on the next line such as **to confide**.) I'm getting worried about him, y'know Biff? (If the actor is

confiding he would be motivated to stop the push-ups and move toward Biff. This might cause Biff, still withdrawing, to move away and perhaps go toward the bed.)

HAPPY (still with the action to confide, which would result in following Biff to the beds): No, I've driven with him. He sees all right. He just doesn't keep his mind on it. (Since he gets no response from Biff, the action might change into **to amuse**.) I drove into the city with him last week. He stops at a green light and then it turns red and he goes.

BIFF (with action **to dismiss** and activity of lying down): Maybe he's color-blind.

HAPPY (perhaps the action on this next line would become **to discover** as Happy is learning something about his brother—Biff is still sour on his Dad): Pop? Why he's got the finest eye for color in the business. You know that.

BIFF (action **to withdraw**): I'm going to sleep.

And this is the end of the beat, after which in the next beat Happy would have to work a bit harder to pursue his need to win Biff, so in the smoking that follows he might use **to lure** and then **buddy up**, etc., motivating Biff to begin to respond as he reaches the next beat with: "Why does Dad mock me all the time?"

Now of course this is 1 out of a possible 30 ways to start the scene. Keeping the same outlines for the characters, and even the same *jump ball* action choices, we might change the activities, starting with Biff withdrawing into his bed and Happy dribbling a basketball. We might change the jump ball actions with the same needs, giving Biff the action **to search** with the activity of pacing and Happy the action **to please** with the activity of fixing the beds, turning down the covers, etc. I cite these only as examples of the possibilities. I do not, however, advise putting your actors through too many changes in this early rehearsal process just for the sake of the exploration of possibilities, as you will only succeed in confusing and irritating them. You should have a pretty good idea of what you want to start with. Only the dreaded blank look in the eye of the actor, questions from or suggestions offered by the actors, or a perception on your part that what you thought might work needed to be rethought should necessitate further exploration.

Whatever you choose, remember that you must allow for the climb to the top of the arc of the scene so you must be careful not to start at a level so high that you have no place to go and no way to build. The stronger actions, such as incite, plead, accuse, threaten, agonize, and so on, should be saved and used as means to increase the dramatic tension as the scene progresses toward the top of the arc.

In my classes I love to astonish the students by showing them visibly how much power they can have as directors and how easy it is to set the whole thing on the wrong course if all the preparation has not been accomplished carefully. To illustrate this, after working in the manner described earlier with two actors, I will change the needs and actions completely, while retaining exactly the same text and making arbitrary (and completely off-the-wall) choices.

For example: HAPPY: Life need: **to prove himself superior**. Scene
    need: **to destroy Biff**. Action: **to belittle**.
BIFF: Life need: **to overcome inadequacy**. Scene need: **to get love**.
    Action: **to show off**.

If we were to put Biff in front of the mirror with the activity of look-ing at his body and the action of showing off, with Happy stretched out on the bed watching him, you can imagine how the scene would start off in a totally different and probably utterly wrong direction. Often when trying this little demonstration with the actors continuing the moment-to-moment from there, the results become outrageous or uproariously funny. The point is clear, and once again the writers quake as they begin to realize how much power the director and actors have over that text that the writers have so painstakingly created.

How do we avoid making the wrong choices and sending each scene off in the wrong direction? At the risk of boring you, I repeat, *it's the throughline* that we have constructed carefully from the text that we must start with and which we must refer to constantly. The life needs of the characters derive from it and all other choices derive from the life needs.

Another device you might find useful in shaping the scene is to find a one or two word label for it that will remind you of what you want to accomplish, what station the scene is on the journey of the line. For example, you might label this first Biff/Happy encounter *the reconnect* scene. Sometimes it's a *sniffing* scene, as in two dogs who meet for the first time, which you might use for the first Conrad/Psychiatrist scene, or *the revelation* which would perhaps label the last Conrad/Psychiatrist scene. Taking care to follow all the steps described earlier should protect you from going too far astray.

With film and television, given the constraints of time, the rehearsal process must be tightly condensed. There is less time for trial and error and the experimentation that might produce invention and discovery. (When I directed the 1-hour daytime drama <u>Another World</u> there was a 2-hour rehearsal in the morning and another one midday for a show that was half the length of a feature!) Thus the director and actors must work specifically and quickly to set the shape of a scene. Everyone involved must have done his/her homework and, while retaining a degree of openness to ideas, be ready to make choices. This is where this shorthand actors' language vividly reveals its usefulness in paring down the time it takes for communication between actors and directors. There is simply no time for long discussions or trial and error. The prose exchange of descriptive paragraphs that we learned as children in elementary school can be and certainly is used by many to get the job done. But at what cost of time, money, and result?

Since there is the opportunity in film to continue the selection of choices during the editing process, many directors will use a succession of different takes of a shot to try out both actors' and director's ideas for the use of possible actions and activities. This is only possible if the budget is expansive, as it can also prove to be a very costly way of working. One of the concerns I have about the Strasberg approach is that it seems to encourage actors to rely so heavily on the feelings, instinct, and inspiration of the moment that no two takes are alike. Often no specific choices are made and the aim is to react "in the moment" so that what was arrived at in rehearsal may never appear in a take. Or each take is a rehearsal. This approach can produce some amazingly truthful and compelling dramatic moments, as well as some brilliant performances as real as life itself. However, like much of life itself, it might lack shape or structure and have no particular arc. It can become what I call a *flatliner* with the audience playing the role of voyeur, making both the director's and editor's jobs in the editing phase of cutting it all together into a cohesive whole not only daunting but extremely expensive. If you want to work this way you will surely get some wonderful footage, but make sure you have unlimited editing time and/or a multimillion dollar budget!

Another aspect of film that needs to be taken into consideration is the fact that often scenes are both rehearsed and shot out of sequence (as was likely the case in the Conrad/Psychiatrist scenes in <u>Ordinary People</u>, which for scheduling purposes were probably addressed one after the other within the same several weeks).

Therefore the continuity of choice is as important as the continuity of shots. The labeling of actions and needs is a huge help in guiding the actor as to where he/she is in the script and reminding the actor about what might have been discovered weeks before in a rehearsal. Thus the overall design and structure of the scene, as well as that of the whole script, is preserved.

The theatre rehearsal process poses another set of circumstances, in some way the opposite of the film experience. In this situation a Strasberg-trained actor might offer you a whole menu of possibilities and with time to indulge the actor, valuable discoveries might be made. However, ultimately that actor must be able to nail down choices or that actor will drive fellow actors insane in their efforts to constantly adjust to the barrage of ever-changing moment-to-moment feelings and instincts.

REHEARSAL SCHEDULE

Some directors want to spend the whole first week, or at the very least several days, discussing the play as a whole and the specifics of the individual characters. Some like to submit to the actors a page or two of written back story for their characters so they can add the material to their homework. For myself, I prefer to use the first day or two for general discussion about script and character and address the specifics of character as we work on each scene. As in film, I like to get the actors up on their feet functioning and behaving within the outlines of the characters to find the behavior and the moment-to-moment truth of the scenes. And the union rules that allow for 8-hour days with a break for lunch, 5 days a week afford the luxury of being able to take the time to experiment, try different things, stop for questions or suggestions, etc.

Although the actual rehearsal process of discussing the throughline, discussing and choosing needs, and selecting a jump ball action for each actor to start the scene is the same as what I've outlined for film, the time frame overall for a typical straight play (i.e., Death of a Salesman) might be something like this:

First week: Days 1 and 2, Read-Through. Discuss play, throughline, and life needs and back story character details. Answer actors' questions. Remainder of week, begin scenes in Act I selecting scene needs as you go.

Second week: Finish scenes in Act 1 and have rough run-through
of Act 1 with notes. Begin scenes in Act 2.

Third week: Finish scenes in Act 2 and have rough run-through of
Act 2 with notes.

Fourth week: First and second days, A.M.: Have stop–start run
throughs of whole play followed by notes; P.M.: Clean up
trouble spots and have stop–start run through and notes.
Third day: No stop run-throughs and notes.

Fourth day to Opening: Run-throughs, Dress rehearsal, cue-to-cue
Tech rehearsal, Tech/Dress, previews followed by notes.

Of course the schedule described is just one of many ways to
approach the task of mounting the production of a play. The nature
and demands of the material are a major factor in deciding when
and how you want to rehearse. However, one of the main things to
remember is the health and well-being of your actors. Often entry-
level directors in nonunion projects in both film and theatre will
work relentlessly long into the night. You might find this to be
totally counterproductive; the combination of the stress of impend-
ing performance together with overwhelming fatigue are a sure
prescription for compromised immune systems. One case of the flu
is then spread throughout the company and your wonderfully vital
cast turns soggy right before your horrified eyes. So watch your
actors carefully for signs of wear and tear. Just as tension reduces
the blood supply to the brain, so does the buildup of lactic acid
manufactured by fatigue slow down the entire instrument.
Directors tend to be intensely single-minded during the rehearsal
period, thinking solely about the fulfillment and success of the
project and forgetting to tend to the health of the team in their
earnest desire to get the job done. Consider this a word to the wise.

In the rehearsal process you are, in effect, playing the actor's
instrument as in the metaphor of the conductor and the orchestra
used previously. Concentrate on getting the notes down first and
then proceed to the fine-tuning.

If an actor has difficulty with an action choice you suggest, try
eliciting the response you want by giving the other actor an action
choice that might necessitate that response. For example, if you
want actor #1 to ward off actor #2, suggest to actor #2 that he/she
keep invading actor #1's space, which would motivate the action
you're suggesting. If the actors seem stuck in choices you want to
discard, try having them abandon the text and instead pursue their

needs and moment-to-moment actions speaking only in alphabet letters or numbers. This sometimes helps the actors erase what you don't want and enables them to start with a clean page.

Identify the transitions both emotional- and thought-wise that the actors must make in the course of the scene and allow them to take the moments necessary to make those transitions in the rehearsal process. Don't worry about pacing or rhythm as you can always tighten things up later in the run-throughs or the shoot.

In general, my rule of thumb is an expectation of seeing about one-half or at best two-thirds of what is arrived at in rehearsal when we get to performance or the shoot due to the presence of an audience or camera and the resulting tension in the actors. Often a student will respond to a critique about missing elements with the reply "well, we talked about that" or "it was there in rehearsal, but not today." Unfortunately, talking about choices will not help the actors as much as having them actually do that which is suggested and then labeling it for future reminder. The less talk and the more doing the better. The director can then refer to his/her notes and be there with the reminder of the choices (*needs and verbs only!*) for key moments before the scene is played or shot.

USE OF IMPROVISATION

My students often raise questions about the use of improvisation both in rehearsal and during actual shooting. Should one use it to help the actors find the realism of the character or the scene? Should one shoot improvised scenes? Shouldn't one emulate brilliant directors like John Cassevetes, who seemed to be shooting entirely improvised features (the truth is that for the most part his work was completely scripted), or, more recently, Mike Leigh, who improvised with his actors for 6 weeks or more to get the scripts for what became the highly regarded films <u>Secrets and Lies</u> and <u>Nora Drake</u>? The question of whether to use improvisation as something other than a classroom exercise comes up more frequently than most others. The truth is, there are no pat answers, as I believe it is a matter of individual preference; it can be useful for some and counterproductive for others. Some actors love to use it. Other actors dislike or even loathe it as a process.

Unfortunately, there are those directors who use improvisation as a way to fill in the gaps of their own preparation and homework by getting the actors to do their work or, in a state of discontent about the script, think that the actors might improve upon the writing with their own improvised dialogue. Or, as in the case of a Mike Leigh, they get the actors to start the writing so that they can, in their auteur hats, then give it the shape and structure that a screenplay or play requires. Most often, the director assumes that he is helping the actor make a connection to the character or find a personalization. In my opinion, these are dangerous paths to follow. In the first place, an actor is not necessarily a writer and while an actor may be able to invent dialogue and behavior that will communicate his own truth, it might not be that of the character. In the second place, actors are working within their individual perceptions and cannot (and indeed should not) step back for a sense of the whole. In the third place, there is no way that, left to their own devices as they improvise, actors can supply the moment to moment that will create the arc of the scene, much less the arc of the play or screenplay. As for connecting to the character, one hopes that your actors, selected through a rigorous casting process, have the craft to do this work on their own time as part of their own homework.

However, all this being said, I have found ways to use improvisation constructively, although I must confess I still believe that it is a device to be used only when the actor is stuck, you are stuck, the writer is dead or otherwise unavailable, or you are working with very young children. The caveat is that I believe *it should be used with the actors pursuing their chosen life and scene needs for the characters* so that they are in the characters' mode of behavior, not their own.

Of course there are examples that argue against my distaste for improvisation as a working tool. Certainly Leigh's work is successful. I'm reminded of a play entitled <u>A Hatful of Rain</u>, written by Michael Gazzo in 1955, which seems to endure and often surfaces in actors' scene classes to this day. I understand it was born of improvisation at the Actors Studio in its early days. Although not revived much, it was a hit in its day and seems to have an extended life. And I'm sure there are many individual examples of the technique's usefulness, but to me they are the exceptions rather than the rule. If you do your homework, hire skilled actors, and collaborate successfully with them using their language, my feeling is that you won't need to call upon your actors' writing skills and use up their energy finding the moment-to-moment truth by this means.

Actually, the use of these and other devices utilized to help write or rewrite a script seems more prevalent in film than in theatre. No doubt this is because of the difference between the two in the perception of the director's role. In film, at the point at which the screenplay has been surrendered by the writer, the director becomes, in effect, the second writer. Once having put the elements together, the director has total control over the finished product, (especially if that director has final cut) and the writer, much to his woe, has been left behind. (How many names of writers of famous screenplays can you remember?) The theatre is a very different story. We still refer to "the Miller play" or "the Stoppard play." Although rarely exercised, playwrights have veto power over everything from director to casting to script changes. This is because the Dramatist Guild has protected them in their standard contract.

My personal preference, probably due to having roots in the theatre, always leans toward collaboration with a writer other than myself whenever possible. Writing and directing are two very different disciplines and I think it is the rare genius who can be excellent at both. I've always believed that two perspectives are better than one and welcome the input of a skilled writer.

NUDITY AND SEX

In recent years nudity and graphic sex have become more and more prevalent in both film and theatre. In the theatre, it seemed to flourish after what was considered the innovative introduction of naked bodies on stage in shows such as Hair (1967) and Oh, Calcutta! (1969). At present, full frontal nudity extending even to the male body, as in The Full Monty, hardly creates a stir. The motion picture code that governs filmmaking once insisted that two people in bed together must each have one foot on the floor. It is now sufficiently relaxed so as to allow not only naked bodies but also graphically explicit sex scenes. In either medium, the planning and rehearsal of these scenes present specific challenges.

The theatre rehearsal with its advantage of time gives actors an opportunity to get to know one another and the director and to get comfortable enough to build the necessary trust. Because the proscenium usually offers a degree of separation from the audience and that distance makes it difficult to be as specific with intimate detail as is possible with the magnifying lens of a camera, the staging of these scenes can be arrived at with the collaboration and organic involvement of the actors. One must be sure to factor in the degree of difficulty in the rehearsal schedule so that the work can be done slowly, patiently, and with respect for the level of stress imposed on the actors. It is assumed of course that in the casting process the actors have been advised of the nature and amount of onstage nudity you will require and that their willingness and ability to collaborate have been established.

In the filming of scenes containing nudity and sex, there is even more necessity for sensitivity. An actor in this situation experiences stress about many things: Will my body look good? Will the other actor like me? Will I like the other actor? (They may have met for the first time that morning if you haven't had the read through.) Will the whole crew be watching? Will I make a fool of myself? As opposed to theatre where the length of exposure only lasts as long as the run of the play, the actor is intensely aware that what is in the film is indelibly preserved.

One way to ensure that most important element of trust is to be sure you are fully prepared. Sex scenes, like fight and action scenes, must be choreographed carefully step by step, just as you would a ballet. Keeping in mind the life and scene needs of the characters, and for film where you might put the camera, you must design a plan for the movement, leaving it flexible enough to be able to accommodate the responses of the actors. My advice is that you do not wait for the inspiration of the moment with these scenes. It is true that the actors will need a certain amount of freedom, but you can help by providing them with a base from which to begin the creation of the moment to moment. You can also make them more comfortable by clearing the set or rehearsal hall of everyone except those whose presence is absolutely necessary.

FIGHT AND ACTION SCENES

With fight scenes it is also essential to be meticulously prepared with choreography. Sometimes it is necessary to break down the moves as specifically as step one, step two, etc. Here it is not only a question of mounting a believable event, it is also a potentially high-risk situation. The actors' safety must be primary and the director must be constantly aware that there is always the potential for an emotionally involved actor to cross the line and get carried away. Some actors are trained in fight skills such as falls, faking punches, fencing, etc. Others have two left feet. Again, this is information about the actors that must be obtained during the casting process. In any case, your preparation must be as detailed as it would be for a ballet. If the script calls for complex fight scenes I would recommend a fight choreographer and, in the case of film, stunt doubles be included even in the lowest of budgets. The time saved and injury prevented will save you money in the long run.

REHEARSING CHILDREN

The rehearsal of children presents yet another special set of circumstances with which the director must cope. There is such a difference in what one might expect from age group to age group that it is difficult to offer generalizations as to how to deal with them. However, there are certain things to note that are pretty universal. For one thing, understand that the attention span of children is considerably shorter than that of most adults. The most negative element to avoid is boredom. When you are rehearsing with children, try to arrange the schedule so that they can get in, do their scene or scenes, and leave. The younger children will have a parent or nanny with them. This can be helpful or intrusive and, as discussed in the casting chapter, you must watch for the too-helpful ones that go over the scripts with the children. Children learn quickly, but because they are working intuitively and can't be expected to have a developed craft, they tend to go into sing-song patterns with constant repetition so beware of too much rehearsal or overly helpful parents or nannies. It is preferable, if possible, to maintain a separate space somewhere on the premises for younger children, within calling distance but separate from the rehearsal area. Provide a supply of age-appropriate toys. As suggested previously, this is one case where I do think improvisation might be useful. Children have wonderful imaginations, their responses are pure and uninhibited, and they seem to embrace improvisation as a fun game. In sum, working with children is another special circumstance and your rehearsal schedule, especially in the case of film, should allow ample time to deal with it.

The ultimate goal in the rehearsal process is to give the actors the security gained by identifying and labeling so that when they get in front of the audience or the camera they can let it all go and just play it. It is my contention, and I think most directors will agree with me, that the rehearsal period can be the most rewarding, creative, and joyous part of the whole process of making a film or mounting a play. If you do your preparation and casting well, you are sure to have a good time.

9

The Actor and the Camera

Since I do believe that the process of directing actors in both theatre and film is basically the same, I haven't made much of a distinction between the two disciplines. But now we come to a step in the process of making a film that includes a special demand on actors and director: the translation of the work to the camera.

The introduction of the camera to the process places a huge demand on the director's attention and can become a compelling distraction. There is so much detail to consider in terms of both technical and aesthetic aspects of the camera's contribution to the total result that often at this point the director is forced to abandon the actors and focus attention on the camera's role in photographing that which has been arrived at in rehearsal in a way that most clearly communicates the director's throughline. At this point the collaborative process centers on the relationship between the director and the director of photography (usually referred to as the DP) as choices are made and often, regrettably, this transfer of attention prevails throughout the shoot.

The thousands of details associated with working with the camera—lighting, design of shots, storyboards, choices of angles, use of lenses, framing, overall composition, special effects, etc. and in general the total translation pictorially of all that we have discussed up to this point—are voluminous enough to fill a very large separate book. There are many excellent books on the subject of the camera and I urge you to investigate them. (The Graduate Film Division of Columbia University's School of the Arts where I teach offers separate disciplines: Directing, which addresses the use of the camera and the entire filmmaking process, and Directing Actors, which is the course this book reflects. Each has its own faculty and in this way the students get in-depth instruction in all aspects of the work.) This chapter will confine our attention to the relationship between the actor and the camera, and I will offer a few suggestions that might help the director enhance the actors' performances.

CATCH THE DETAILS

It is obvious that all the best work in rehearsal is of little use if the results don't appear on camera. Just as the actors form the conduit that carries your throughline, so must the camera relay all the behavioral information to the film audience. When looking at a cut of a short film by a student that has rehearsed in my class, I often find myself searching in vain for the interesting, creative moments we saw in those class rehearsals. One constantly hears actors complaining that what they thought was their best work never made it to the screen. It is true that, in the editing process, at times it is necessary to alter or surrender seemingly telling moments for a variety of reasons. But it is also true that directors often become so distracted with the thousands of technical demands that surface during a shoot that they either overlook or forget the valuable detail that the actors are contributing. It is therefore important to make careful notes during the rehearsal process so that they can be referred to as you storyboard or design shots. It is also important to watch your actors carefully during a take so as to catch any bit of valuable behavior that might surface on the spur of the moment. Many directors rely heavily on viewing the tape hook-up during a take. It is often placed at a distance from the actors, which sometimes causes the actors distress. Many actors like to feel the director's presence, that they are performing for the director. I think it helps to stay near the camera to let them know you're there. (If necessary, review the shot after the take.)

THE CAMERA AS ACTOR

Try to think of the camera as an actor on the team. In a documentary the camera is usually objective, i.e., it watches the action from outside the event. It reveals fact. But in narrative film the aim is to involve the audience in the story to the point where it loses sight of the camera and enters into the story as a participant. If the audience is aware of the camera, then it knows it is watching make-believe. *Directors who like to show off by choosing unexpectedly clever or daring shots that interrupt the narrative flow are, in my opinion, shooting themselves in the foot.* Unless these shots become an integral part of the story, it simply reminds us that there is a camera, a director telling it what to do, and that it is all fakery. In allowing the camera to become an actor in the scene, I am suggesting that *the camera's movement be motivated by and follow the actors* rather than having the actors move for the camera, thereby making its perspective a subjective rather than an objective one. This approach necessitates rehearsing first to allow the actors to find the movement motivated by the pursuit of their needs and actions and then following the rehearsal each day with the work of sketching storyboards that will define the camera positions and moves. Of course, sometimes there is the necessity of placing the actor or asking the actor to *hit the marks* when a specific location, lighting, or other demand arises. But hopefully you can keep that need down to a bare minimum as it will limit the actor's freedom and ability to find the behavior of the character.

ESTABLISH GEOGRAPHY

Unless you are going for some special effect and want to create a puzzle for the audience or keep them guessing and/or in suspense, it is important to establish the geography of a scene. The old tradition of starting with a master shot and then going in for angles and close-ups, now somewhat archaic, was based on sound logic. An involved audience needs to know something about the environment that surrounds the actors. If you don't give it to them, they will be distracted, taking their attention away from what the actors are doing to figure it out. Just as you don't want the audience to be thinking about their laundry list because they've anticipated what's coming, you don't want them to lose the actors while they attempt to work out visual puzzles. Be as creative in your shot design as you can, but remember that both the visual cues *and* the actors playing the characters are the conduits for your throughline.

CHOICE OF SHOT

The choice of type of shot—master, wide two shot, tighter two shot, over the shoulder, chest or shoulder high shot, close-up, tracking shot, etc.—can enhance the performance of the actor and help define the scene and build the arc. The nature of the material, the position and purpose of the scene in regard to the throughline, and the needs of the characters must all be considered in making the choices. I refer you again to my favorite example. Look at the first scene between the psychiatrist and Conrad in Ordinary People and then go to each of the successive scenes between those two characters in that same office. Notice how the director keeps the characters in single shots and very wide two shots with a table between them in the initial scene, defining their relationship at that point. The camera allows us to see Conrad's body as he twitches and fidgets. Now look at the scenes that follow. With each new visit, and as they begin to close in on the problem, the singles become tighter, the two shots are closer as the table separating them disappears. The camera moves into the actors with each revelation, bringing the characters together, until finally we see them in extreme close-up. The trust has been established and the breakthrough occurs. Watch how the lighting complements the design of shots, with fairly normal daylight to begin with that darkens gradually as the intensity heightens until we get the final chiaroscuro effect as the doctor digs deep. The camera is an actor in the scenes, and the light design accompanies the camera's performance.

Discussions of choice of shots or which character the camera should see often arise during the edit. It is at this point that I hear the phrase "who drives the scene?" used as a yardstick of judgment. However, I prefer that the choices be guided more by the understanding of what station the scene is on the journey of the throughline, how the protagonist carries the story forward, and what the scene is about (as in the one or two word labels referred to previously). Remember, sometimes the camera should be on the silent character rather than the one with the most dialogue.

Sometimes it is useful during the rehearsal process to make yourself the camera and place your body where you think the camera might be placed. Then, as the actors find the movement in the scene, you will be able to judge what the camera will see as it follows the actors from a given position. This can be useful in the drawing of the storyboards that follow that rehearsal.

THE EYES OF THE ACTOR

The tool kit of the actor contains the use of the body, the voice, the language, the memory, the imagination, the intelligence, and the life experience, all of which combine to make the instrument. If you deny the actor any one of these components, you are, in effect, putting a mute on the instrument or hobbling it. *The two eyes of the actor are among the most important conveyers of thought, emotion, and/or reaction.* Yet so many directors choose to show us the actor in profile much of the time, and regrettably at some of the most important moments. Try this experiment: Take a still photograph of one side of an actor's face. Then take another still photograph of the other side of the same actor's face. Lay them side by side. As it is extremely rare that the human face has perfect symmetry, you will see two surprisingly different expressions! Which is the one you wanted to convey? *By limiting the audience access to only one eye, the director limits the actor's ability to fully communicate the experience of the moment.* Of course, there are situations that demand that the actors be placed vis á vis, such as an embrace or a face-to-face confrontation. But whenever and wherever possible, I beg you to give your actors a break and place your camera so that we can at least get a piece of the second side of the face and see both eyes. It is probably this awareness of the difference in sides of the face that creates the apocryphal stories about film stars who insist on being photographed only from their "best" side.

CLOSE-UPS

Recently I've noticed what seems to be a trend in the overuse of extreme close-ups in film, often at the sacrifice of both interaction and environmental influence. It seems that television with its comparatively small screen, the proliferation of all that is digital, and the growing use of video hook-ups on film sets have encouraged the tendency to use more and more close-ups. I am constantly reminding my film students to take into consideration how a close-up will appear on the much larger motion picture screen This problem is exacerbated by the fact that in most classroom situations the student work is viewed on tiny DVD or VHS monitors. Personally I find it very jarring to be suddenly confronted with a close-up that pops up following a master or wide shot for no apparent reason.

Unless the camera move is motivated in some way by an actor's move or a specific action or text demand, it once again reminds the audience of the camera's existence. Rather than enhancing the actor's moment, it becomes a distraction. In addition, too often the close-up gives us little or no information as to the subtext of the character because the actor hasn't been helped by the director to choose the appropriate subtext action for the shot. Often it is a shot of the actor's reaction to another character or an event, but if that moment isn't defined with a clear action choice, we are limited to viewing the face as one would a painted portrait. When it is the face of an extremely beautiful actor, like an Angelina Jolie or a Brad Pitt, there is a certain aesthetic pleasure to be derived from the shot, but it hardly advances the story. (The film Brokeback Mountain released in December 2005, directed by Ang Lee with a sparely written screenplay by Larry McMurtry, provides a good example of how meaningful silent reaction shots can advance the story.) Therefore use careful selectivity in choosing your close-ups. Make sure the actor has a specific action choice even if it is a silent reaction shot and keep in mind the size of the screen.

NUMBER OF TAKES

Questions always arise in regard to the number of takes an actor can sustain while still preserving the *illusion of the first time* which is our goal. This is a huge variable. Some actors want to keep going until they feel they've hit the truth of the shot. Others chafe at the thought of more than two or three takes. Liv Ullman once said in an interview that she believed the first take was always the best one because it was the most intuitive. As I've discussed in a previous chapter, there are actors who will give you new ideas and a different performance on each take, resulting in wide variety and time-consuming multiple choice in the edit. So much depends on the nature of what is being shot, the degree of technical difficulty surrounding it, the number of ideas your DP (Director of Photography) has and wants to try, the number of light, shadow, and sound glitches that might occur, and, certainly not least, consideration of the time your budget allows. It is impossible to generalize about numbers. My experience has been that if you follow our approach through the preplanning, casting, and rehearsal stages, you'll know what you need and you'll know how to get the actors there quickly. With perhaps one extra for protection, you should be able to get what you want in three or four takes barring technical disasters. Too often I see directors continue to shoot take after take because they aren't sure what they will want when they get to the edit stage. I'm reminded of the film <u>The Landlord</u> (1970) once again. Hal Ashby, who was the gifted editor who helped make <u>In the Heat of the Night</u> an Academy Award winner, was directing his first feature. He shot enough film for two pictures, knowing full well that at that point, editing was his strong suit and he could make crucial choices and shape the film in the editing process. The producer of the film was Norman Jewison, director of <u>In the Heat of the Night</u> thus Ashby was indulged with a lot of budget leeway.

COVERAGE

One way to ensure the preservation of the actors' good work is to get plenty of coverage (shooting one beat from various angles or in a variety of ways). I know that word comes up frequently in camera classes, but here I use it in relationship to the actors and the means by which you can allow yourself sufficient choice when you get to the edit phase of the work. It is true that there is often the obstacle of limited time, particularly in low-budget and student films, but the failure to get sufficient coverage can wreak havoc later on.

"Do you have a tighter reaction shot here so I can see the expression on the actor's face when she says she's leaving him?" I will ask the student as we view a rough cut. "No," sighs the student regretfully. "I knew I should have it but we had to leave the location—we'd run out of time."

This is a regrettable and all too common error. Factor in the time needed to get as much coverage as possible in your day-to-day planning. Never lose sight of what you might want the audience to see at any given moment, as well as what you need to convey to get your throughline across.

LOCATIONS

An exterior location is even more of a challenge for obvious reasons. All of the surrounding elements affect not only the actor's concentration, but also his/her awareness and self-consciousness in the presence of the camera. These in turn may also affect the actor's memory. Here again it is partly a question of budget as to how well you can protect the performances. The nature of the scene being shot, the level of experience of the actors, and the kind of environment surrounding the work will be determining factors as to how much attention you must give this issue. With exteriors it is important to provide sufficient crowd control to protect the actors. Either on set or off set, a quiet separate space must be provided for the actors, whether it be in the form of dressing rooms, nearby trailers, or simply a room in an adjacent building.

ADJUSTING TO THE CAMERA

Take into consideration the fact that each actor might react differently to the camera, regardless of what you have discovered during the rehearsal process. The more experienced actor is rarely thrown by the presence of the camera and can usually be relied upon to deliver what you might expect. But even here there is a variable: the rehearsal environment is usually a pretty private affair, where everything is designed to accommodate the actor's ability to focus. The set is peopled with an array of strangers, many of whom are noisily pursuing their assigned tasks. Each actor reacts to the addition of the camera in his own way. Some withdraw into themselves as the insecurity of the moment results in a form of hiding and the action choices seem to lessen in intensity. Others react conversely and seem to be concerned about projecting with clarity, punching up the intensity of the choices.

Often you might find that an actor who is primarily theatre oriented and might be facing the camera for the first time appears disturbingly overprojected for the camera's penetrating eye. The necessity of projecting across the proscenium sets certain reflexes in the theatre-based actor. My advice to directors is to keep your antenna up, particularly when you are working with primarily theatre-oriented actors. *Do not let all the distractions of a shoot rob you of your perception and attention to the actor*. The problem is easy to fix, with the use of my approach, by simply adjusting the level of intensity of the action choice. But be warned, do not attempt to help the situation this way: "John, it's too big. Do less." Do it this way: "John, instead of **threatening** him in this moment, **intimidate** him."

Seemingly small adjustments can change the whole thrust of the character's needs, presenting the director with a rude surprise upon viewing the tapes or the dailies. Thus it is essential that the director overcome the thousands of other distractions brought to bear during a shoot that conspire to take your mind off the actor. This is the occasion where the shorthand vocabulary can be most useful. A brief reminder to the actor of the needs or an action choice found previously, and noted in your script, in a given moment is usually all it takes to get the scene back to what you arrived at in rehearsal.

It is the point at which the actors meet the camera that I believe the stress level is the highest. As I keep reminding you, tension reduces the blood supply to the brain. At a time when you want your actors to be their most imaginative and creative, circumstances conspire to inhibit, if not seriously limit, the actors' ability to function. I was impressed by his awareness of this when the actor/director Clint Eastwood mentioned, in an interview about his directing, that he doesn't even like to shout "action!" to start the work as he wants to keep the actors as relaxed as possible. I suspect one of the reasons that the directors I mentioned in a previous chapter who have had background as actors are so successful is because they have a visceral understanding of the kinds of stress placed upon actors in the actual shooting of a scene and are sensitive to the actors' needs in this regard.

EMOTIONAL DEMAND

A heavy emotional demand in a scene presents a special challenge, particularly when the script calls for a fraught subtext or an outburst of tears or anger. Every actor has a different way of preparing for this, but it is up to the director to make sure that the actor is allowed sufficient quiet on the set and time to prepare. I'm reminded of a recent Inside the Actors Studio segment in which Jane Fonda told of some of her experiences in shooting On Golden Pond with her father, the late, great Henry Fonda. She found one scene so close to the reality of their relationship that she was moved to tears every time she worked on it in rehearsal. It seemed she couldn't stop crying. But when she was confronted with the moment of truth in front of the camera, "I was dry," she said in a tone of horror. Fortunately, with the use of her craft and the urging of costar Katherine Hepburn, who was lurking off camera, she was able to rescue the moment. *You might find it useful to consider sched-uling the demanding emotional scenes late in the day when the actor is likely to be more tired and therefore more vulnerable.* Fatigue often low-ers our resistance and makes the emotional life more accessible.

NONACTORS

Nonactors who have been hired for their "look" or authenticity, entry-level actors with no camera experience, and children offer the biggest challenge, particularly in the adjustment period in the early stages of shooting. The temptation to look straight at the cam-era, particularly with children, seems overwhelming. Whether it be conscious or subconscious awareness of the position of the camera, the actor will often *cheat* toward it no matter where he/she is placed. It can take all of a director's craftiness to get believable per-formances from those in this group. It is not only a challenge, it is also a huge time waster. It is the main reason that I prefer to avoid working with nonactors and to seek, in the casting phase, profes-sional actors with training and craft or, in the case of children, high intelligence and the ability to concentrate.

IMBALANCE

Sometimes you might encounter a situation in which there is an imbalance between the performances of the actors in a given take. One actor may be fine in takes one and two but the other actor or actors are weak. In takes three and four the weak actors are better but the other actor has lost the edge that made the performance great. This is where those little one word action verbs can jump to your rescue. If you are fluent enough in the vocabulary it will only take a minute to fine-tune each actor or recall the successful choices so that the balance can be restored. If you are confronted with the problem too late, i.e., in the edit, then a compromise must be made and I would advise choosing the best take of the protagonist, who, after all, is the one moving the line forward. In any case, *whenever possible let the actors know why you are doing another take even when it doesn't require an additional direction.* A good percentage of the time it is a technical reason that has nothing to do with the actors and they need to know that.

PREPARATION IS EVERYTHING

The best way to ensure sufficient time with your actors on the set and a successful shoot is to **be meticulously prepared**. In view of the emergencies, surprises, and questions that are part of the routine hour-by-hour demands that accompany the director's work, the more problems you can anticipate and eliminate through careful and diligent homework, the better off you and your actors will be. Although collaboration is of the essence, do not wait for or trust the impulses of your actors or DP to get you through. Rehearse constructively, do your homework thoroughly, be the first one on the set, treat your actors with respect and caring, revere your DP and AD (assistant director), and you will sail through.

Sidney Lumet, who has directed many successful films and collected many awards, among them the Academy's Lifetime Achievement Award, has had a reputation for bringing in his films on time and on budget. I suspect that is because he selects his casts carefully, insists on rehearsal, nurtures his actors, and has a background in both theatre and live television. Because of the demand of the latter experience, he is always carefully prepared and seems to cut the picture in his head as he works, making untold numbers of takes unnecessary. For me, he is the kind of director that can provide an actor's Eden.

10
Film and Theatre: Similarities and Differences

The general misconception held by most laypeople and some professionals seems to be that there must be a difference between the crafts of directing and acting in theatre and those in film. The belief is that there are stage actors and screen actors, film directors and theatre directors. I don't agree with this. It is true that some actors and directors have more experience in one or the other form and thus have to make adjustments or add to their awareness of certain elements in crossing over. But it is my contention that the basics of the crafts remain the same. However, it is true that the skilled actor does not necessarily automatically become the skilled director nor should one assume that the skilled director can also act.

THE LANGUAGE: A SIMILARITY

What is certainly the same, at least in my approach, is the language of communication. Although the director's work calls for an overview of the material and an awareness of the throughline and outlines for each character as opposed to the actor who simply has to focus on his/her own role, the means of communication by which the actor and director collaborate to lift the words off the page and breathe life into them can be the same. My workshops, which always include actors, directors, and yes also writers, all work together with the same approach. The results are testament to the fact that this can be done successfully.

The realities of economic survival demand that both actors and directors be capable of moving with ease from theatre to film or television if they have the desire for a roof over their heads and food on their tables. It is well known among members of our industry that working in the theatre is a luxury ill-afforded if it means taking time from the much more lucrative remuneration offered by film and television. There is frequent mourning by the theatre community over the apparent loss of talented playwrights who have opted for the good life by writing screenplays and who have seemingly deserted the theatre. In the days of what is lovingly called the "golden age" of theatre (the forties, fifties, and sixties), the motion picture industry derived much of its material and talent from the theatre. Plays were purchased from successful runs on Broadway and adapted into films. Actors were discovered in Off-Broadway plays and quickly became stars, As I write this book, it seems the worm is turning: Work initiated in film is adapted for the stage. Actors known entirely for their film work are appearing for the first time on the boards and even directors, some of whom began in the theatre, are either returning to the fold or trying on the experience of directing theatre for the first time. And this is all happening with varying degrees of success or failure.

SIZE: A DIFFERENCE

There are some differences that must be taken into consideration and addressed in the course of the work. The first and most obvious of these is the question of size. We've examined the issue of size of screen in the chapter about the actor and the camera, particularly in the use of close-ups, but here I am referring to another aspect that is almost the opposite concern. It is that in theatre, the presence of a proscenium, or whatever separates the live audience from the actors, demands a certain level of projection. It is not only necessary to be seen and to project the actions and activities clearly, the actors must also be heard and understood in the upper reaches of the balcony. The actors' training therefore must include the ability to retain the truth of their characters while finding a level, often slightly larger than life, that will project that reality to the large watching audience. The camera, conversely, is like a microscope, examining the actor's every move, the slightest twitch. But the quick wink of an eye, so telling on the screen, might be lost to an audience of more than 25 in a theatre environment.

In the previous chapter I've referred to the case where, when working with talented trained actors who have had extensive background in theatre but little or no film experience, my film students have, on viewing their dailies, had a rude surprise. What seemed so right in the protected intimacy of the rehearsal hall suddenly leaps from the screen seeming *pushed* or indicated. What happens is that the actor goes into performance mode in front of the camera and reflexively projects in the manner customary to the theatrical experience. Without realizing the effect that this seemingly slight change might have on the balance between actors, the choice of actions, and so on, the team presses blithely on. It is a sad moment in the editing room when the director realizes that the lack of attention to even the most subtle of changes in the actor's performance might make it necessary to reshoot or, even worse, to settle for something less than desirable.

ADJUSTMENTS

By the same token, when an actor who has come from an exclusively filmic background attempts to do a play, there are several new challenges: There is the necessity to adjust to the fact that there is no microphone hovering an inch away to catch every nuance, that there is no ability to call "cut" and stop when something goes awry, that the entire script has to be memorized, and that the actor has to project the life of the character in every moment on stage, speaking or not, and for everyone in the audience. The introduction of film and TV stars into Broadway and Off-Broadway productions has been increasingly prevalent for obvious economic reasons, making it necessary for directors to be very aware of the necessity of attending to and assisting the actors in making these adjustments.

The text in a theatre piece is usually much fatter; there is more dialogue. In film, so much can be communicated visually. Silence can be illuminated by the visual shot and in high-action films there is even less talk. A filmic scene is usually much shorter than a scene in a play. Thus in theatre the vocal demand increases greatly. Those actors who have had theatre training have usually studied voice production, speech, movement, and, in some acting programs, even circus, which might include juggling and balance exercises. (Everyone was startled recently when Glenn Close attempted to show off her juggling ability on Jay Leno's <u>Tonight Show</u>.) It is tacitly understood that the whole instrument must be ready and able to deliver whatever might be demanded of it. An actor who may have jumped into film work shortly after being discovered, having left limited college or community theatre training to build an auspicious career as a film star, might find the adjustment extremely difficult. Those who have attempted the crossover often come down with that dreaded affliction of actors and singers known as laryngitis. The vocal chords are simply not used to the demand and they protest.

Memory muscles, which haven't been required to recall much more than a beat or two at a time for the camera, struggle with the obligation to learn page after page of dialogue. Sometimes the performance is so subtle that it can't be read past the sixth row. The wise director who is confronted with the necessity of casting an actor in this category should insist that the actor do several months of preproduction classes in both scene study and voice production in preparation for the theatre experience.

The actors' speech patterns and quirks, as well as dialects, present other difficulties to which the director must attend. Here again, film tends to magnify the sibilant or lisping 's' sound and other speech impediments. They can become a comedy device, but if the material is not essentially comedic, it might require significant time devoted to looping or dubbing. Although there is a growing use of amplification in theatre to accommodate actors' inability to project (much to the dismay of the old guard), those small speech difficulties are usually not quite so noticeable.

In the old days, theatre actors were expected to learn what was referred to as "standard stage English." But with the advent of playwrights such as O'Neill, Odets, Williams, Mamet, and Rabe, it has become more about the vernacular and/or *street* dialect and there is no longer any standard. Mainly it is a matter of clarity, of being understood by the audience. In this instance the amazing technology of film has an advantage, the sound track can be cleaned up so the demand on the actor becomes less critical. But the careful director, whether casting for film or theatre, should keep a sharp ear out for anything in the speech that might become a future problem, weighing its importance depending on the medium in which the director is working.

For actors there is also the question of preparation for the needs and emotional state of the character before an entrance or before a shot. In the theatre an actor can prepare in the relative privacy of the dressing room or in the darkness of the wings. In film the actor is often faced with the necessity of preparing amidst an assemblage of busy crew members or on a crowded and noisy thoroughfare. Contrary to popular opinion, not everyone can rate a personal trailer. Particularly in film, the director must be sensitive to the needs of the actor and the necessity of preparing.

Another difference between the two pursuits is the number of people involved in the realization of the project. In both instances, for however long, the team becomes a closely knit family until the show closes or the film is wrapped. In theatre that family is relatively small in size, with the possible exception of the recently imported mega-musical trend. But the number of people overall who are involved in the making of a film is much greater and demands a special skill on the part of the director to act as a unifying force. Many actors appear and disappear from the shoot, often having a shooting schedule lasting 2 weeks out of a total of perhaps 26 weeks of production.

Time Factor

In theatre the actors see each other every night and twice on matinee days for the length of the run, and the director is long gone, leaving the stage manager to maintain the level of the work. This allows for fluidity in the work, and often there will be ongoing development and experimentation with a stage manager keeping a hopefully watchful eye on the overall result. The wise director will check in on the performance periodically to make sure that the integrity of the original production is preserved.

With a film the director prevails until the work is ready for distribution and whatever is in the can or on the tape is preserved, hopefully, forever with all its artistry and/or errors intact. This might be one of the reasons that many stage directors yearn to do film (aside from the difference in financial remuneration of course). It is disheartening to put your energies and talent into a project that at best has such a limited life and then disappears from view except perhaps for an archival tape stored in the Lincoln Center Library Theatre Collection in New York City.

But balance this with the fact that theatre offers instant gratification, whereas a director might have to wait for a year or more to get a response to a film. There is nothing more satisfying and fulfilling than standing in the darkened rear of a theatre and listening to a packed house laugh and cry exactly where you wanted them to. And this can happen as soon as 6 weeks after the start of rehearsal.

AUDIENCE

There is another consideration when examining the differences between theatre and film. Because we as directors are essentially communicators and it is assumed that in our work we have something to say, it is worth noting the difference in size of a potential audience. A successful film, with the possibility of worldwide distribution and its continued life on VHS and DVD, reaches an infinitely larger number of viewers than the longest running play, which even with the possibility of periodic revival and touring is limited in comparison.

In any case, an established director will no doubt find him/herself eventually working in theatre, film, and television during the course of a career, and it is my contention that the approach to working with actors, including the vocabulary of communication and the steps in the preparation process, is basically the same. The actors' craft, regardless of the form, is also basically the same.

As a pioneer in this area, it is heartening to note that the concept of teaching Directing Actors as a separate discipline seems to be proliferating in academia and conservatory training programs. If you learn to become fluent in the approach to the task, you will be able to move with ease among the various forms as far as the actors are concerned, leaving yourself the time and energy to deal with the technical differences inherent in each.

11

What Do the Actors Say?

As I have been saying repeatedly in many different ways, **Listen to your actors at all times!** Assuming that you have done a good job on the casting process and that you've hired good actors, you will find that your actors' instincts, as well as your own, are among the best friends you've got on the project. Most actors, particularly good actors, are intelligent, sensitive, and articulate. They usually have an unerring instinct about what is right for their characters and for themselves as actors. I believe that the reason many actors become directors is that they are weary of the frustrations generated as a result of being ignored by arrogant or overly insecure directors who remain stuck in their own rigidity. Eventually these actors decide to take matters into their own hands.

Do not think that you are losing control if you allow the actors to voice their suggestions or concerns. In actuality you are commanding their respect and trust when they discover that you have enough security to be able to stay open to their ideas. Just as you would listen to advice from your DP as to an angle for a film shot or from your set designer as to the type of furniture needed for a stage set, so should you allow the creative processes of your actors to inform your choices. Remember, the work is being guided and your intent preserved by the all-important throughline, which must be referred to constantly at every step of the way so as to protect your vision. If you've done a careful job on your throughline and everyone on the team is working collaboratively on the realization of that throughline, you can afford to remain open and flexible without danger of losing anything valuable.

In the hope of giving you a bit more insight into what actors think and feel, a sampling from various sources follows—most often from Professor Annette Insdorf's interviews as part of her brilliant series, <u>Reel Pieces</u> which runs every year at the 92nd Street Y in New York City. These excerpted thoughts of film and theatre notables are in responses to interviewers' questions.

Sir Ben Kingsley: Excerpts from <u>Reel Pieces</u>

"What can the director give you that allows you to do your best work? Help me whittle it down. The less I can act the more will come out of the collective subconscious. If you see me doing seven things ask for five, if five ask for three. Help me whittle it down, pare it away.

"The film directors I have loved working with are the ones who have given me a place to stand in which I can be as minimal as I dare and as truthful as possible within the minimalism and then have put the camera in exactly the right place and used exactly the right lens.

"The danger of losing spontaneity isn't one that's encountered too often under the guidance of a good director.

"There is a danger with some directors that they insist on auditioning you for the part once you've got it—day after day after day. Whereas other directors who are more secure and more adult will give you the part because they think you can do it. If he or she overdirects and insists on the finished product or the overly realized character then what the camera never sees is that extraordinary leap from actor to character where the actor is in no-man's land, becoming the character. If the camera catches that moment, the leap out of myself to become the character—that is perfection. If the director has fully organized where he/she wants you to land, how he/she wants you to land. . . . Where have I got go? Where's the leap?

"Working in the theatre has given me stamina, sensitivity, and dependence on my fellow actors.

"Rehearsal in film, if it is in the hands of a skillful director, can pay enormous dividends. But if there is an indolent self-indulgent attitude on the part of the director that says 'impress me,' the actors can sense that. If the motives are good and creative it can be a great process. Rehearsals are like walking the track before you race around it."

Meryl Streep: Excerpts from <u>Reel Pieces</u>

"The first encounter, the reading around the table, is often the most thrilling, exciting interaction that you have in a movie because you never ever have it all in one piece again. You have your little page—half of the pie—every day and you spend laborious hours trying to make it fresh. So that first reading is often thrilling and what you try to get back to in the whole long shoot. And it's all about making a connection and listening and discovering who the person is. What I said about the first reading I feel the same about a play.

"It is most fun in the world to work with Mike Nichols because he works so hard in the process of entertaining everybody, keeping everybody happy. The actors love to work with him because he moves the story and the day through in a way that's productive and inventive. He's very present in the moment and that's all he wants is for it to live right there in front of his eyes. If it does happen there, tears come and he can't control his involvement. That contribution from behind the camera is so disarming because it's a form of energy that you get. He comes in incredibly prepared. He asks 'what are you doing in the scene? What do you want?'

"The longer I do this, the less I understand about the entire process. What is it? Fifty percent fairy dust and fifty percent farm work. It takes stamina and musculature and it's boring—and then there's magic!

"I don't want to be boss. I want to know that the director has that architectural form and the structure is going to hold and I can hurl my entire body into it and it won't break. Actors can't give it to people they don't trust.

"In film you can't let any of the work show. The work precedes (the performance). It's way, way behind. It's like your lunch: it's in your stomach but you don't want to look at it."

Meryl Streep: Excerpt from the American Film Institute magazine, *American Film*

"I think that everybody has everything in them, and that usually directors and casting people see so little of what you have. They see so little of your potential. You have everybody in you. And people who really want to act can access all kinds of horrible things. And that's what we ask actors to do. We want them to channel murderers, and we want to see that played out. There is a need for people to embody these unspeakables and unimaginables. That's the actor's job.

"I hate those meetings where you walk in, sit down, and they just want to have a look at you. Well, then that's all they're going to get—a look at you and a look at you is nothing. You've got to imagine and really see people's work because that is where you'll find out if they can open you up to the hidden world of a character, to the aspects that are never explained.

"What enables you to do your best work as an actor is the trust of the director and the feeling that whatever you come up with, he's going to seriously consider it, weigh it, and believe in you whether or not he agrees with you about the choice that you've made in a scene. That really makes a big difference. It's like being at the piano recital if your parents don't show up, or if they're in the back holding their breath. You feel better when they are there. You feel like you could do things. If your parents are not there, maybe you can do it but it's different. The director is like the parent."

Denzel Washington: Heard on WNET's _Charlie Rose_

Discussion of _Manchurian Candidate_

(Referring to stage directions in the script) "It's not about 'reeling back' or 'screaming.' The character is much too depressed to do those things. I don't like being told how to indicate an emotion. The writer is usually saying 'that's how I would do it.' But I want to find my own way. In having the courage to go with the integrity of my belief I trust that I would be getting the emotional impact. If the writer says 'deeply distressed,' you are forced to perform something instead of being allowed to find the moment."

Glenn Close: Excerpt from _Reel Pieces_

"I have learned a tremendous amount from my directors. I learned the most things I've taken with me from Istvan Zsabo (Mephisto). He had two pages of closely printed back-story—I loved it! He breathes with you. Once I knew I didn't have it and he knew I didn't have it. Instead of panic there was patience. He said, 'It's okay, it's okay . . . we're waiting for the angel.'

"If an actor is doing something and the camera is in the wrong place you don't get it. Knowing where to put the camera to capture what you're doing makes the difference between really communicating and impacting—and not.

"As for rehearsal in film, I prefer to rehearse because I think of acting as a craft although some directors think it's left to chance.

"Trevor Nunn (theatre director) sat around a table for at least a week talking about the research."

Michael Caine: Excerpts from _Reel Pieces_

"I do work in the Stanislavski system.

"A movie star has the duty to supply an entertaining personality which amuses his audience and fans. A movie actor's duty is to disappear into the character. I used to be a movie star. Now I'm a movie actor.

"The rehearsal is the work. The filming is the relaxation.

"A great director will leave you alone until you've started going wrong and then he will put you on the right track with a couple of sentences.

"John Huston said to me: 'Speak faster Michael. He's an honest man.' That summed up the character for me in one sentence, told me what I needed to know about the character. But for the rest of my life it made me suspicious of people who talk slowly, as in Texas where I just shot a film.

"Who said 'dying is easy, comedy is hard'?"

Julianne Moore: Excerpts from <u>Reel Pieces</u>

"Comedy is really so hard. How difficult it is to get it right. People who can create them are astonishing—really smart people.

"I hate to rehearse. On <u>The Hours</u> the three of us were talking and Nicole (Kidman) said she loves to rehearse and Meryl (Streep) was saying 'well sometimes you have to and sometime you don't'—and you hear all three of us talking and having these different methods. And Steven Daltry (director) had to deal with all of us, a cast of a very disparate group of actors with very different working methods. He had to adapt himself to those different methods.

"For me it's important that the director have a vision and be able to communicate it to me in some way. I can then figure out how to get there. I don't want a director to be an acting coach. I just want them to say 'this is how I see the film.'"

Christopher Walken: Excerpts from <u>Reel Pieces</u>

"Movie acting is a kind of science and part of it involves stuff that people don't see when they see the movie. Movie acting is more like rehearsing because you're shooting rehearsal and accidents are great stuff.

"People say there's a difference between movie acting and stage acting, but acting is acting. Getting back on stage is like getting tuned. You tune your instrument.

"Doing Chekhov is my favorite thing. I guess I'm always doing Chekhov!"

John Turturro: Excerpts from <u>Reel Pieces</u>

"Theatre is humbling. If you can do it there you learn the whole thing. You're the editor. It's really the actors' medium. Many times in film you're just a body and you have to struggle to be treated as a person. You have many meetings, costume fittings, etc. but then when you get there, it's hurry up, hurry up. Movie making is expensive. It's a constant state of crisis so you have to find a way to function in it.

"Some directors I've worked with stay behind their monitor. They don't even talk to you. So it's like making love to yourself. It's very lonely. And then you get someone who talks to you. The director and other actors are your only audience."

Kevin Kline: Excerpts from <u>Reel Pieces</u>

"In the theatre you get to be the storyteller every night, but the director has shaped your thinking.

"There are directors in the theatre as well as directors in film who are auteur who make the play or film about their vision. And there are others who collaborate and are interested in the actors' vision as well. And then there are those in between who are auteurs but who bring aboard actors whose vision is malleable enough to fit theirs or whose vision is in sync with theirs. We work with all of those but I always prefer collaboration. But ultimately you do have to surrender a certain amount of control. More so in film because not only are you interpreting the role, you are being further interpreted by the camera, the editing, the music, the montage, etc. You look at a scene that you shot over a week and they cut it in a way and the camera moves and the music comes in and you go 'It's magic! I can't believe it's me!' They made it something wonderful—and that's cinema. It's very exciting to be a part of that."

Jennifer Lopez: From <u>Inside the Actors Studio</u> on BRAVO

"What do I want ideally from a director? I want him to push me, push me."

Michael Douglas: Excerpts from <u>Reel Pieces</u>

"I tend to think that European directors are more removed from the actors. They know they've hired you and if they cast correctly they're not involved in directing you per se. American directors are more concerned with being involved with the acting process.

"I'm a firm believer that everything has to be in sync before we start—we all have to be speaking the same language. I encourage the director to talk through as specifically as possible because we're in such an interpretive art form.

"Normally directors act like patriarchs and they treat actors like children—they treat us like big father.

"Directing is a very lonely job. I have the greatest respect for directors. You get no help from anybody else."

Edward Norton: Excerpts from <u>Reel Pieces</u>

"DeNiro was a big influence on me. A light bulb went off in my head about the job, the craft. The way I had envisioned the scene (in <u>The Score</u>), I would come in blazing and he (DeNiro) would hit back at me really hard. . . . As we got into it I was hitting hard at him and he wasn't coming back with anything like what I was expecting . . . and I had this fear that he wasn't going to give me anything back and was going to leave me hanging and I got very tense. I caught eyes with him and he made this little hand gesture almost like 'hey, I'm right here' and I had this light bulb go off in my head and I realized I'd been thinking about mixing it up with this actor since I was about 11 years old and I'm here doing it with him and I'm not even taking it off him. I'm acting a vision of the scene that I've had as a writer and as a director. I've seen the way I think the scene is supposed to play and I'm not even paying attention to him, what he's actually doing. I said to myself, just chuck it and see what he's doing. And by the time we got to the end of it I thought he was a genius because I realized that he was not failing to respond to me. He was making a choice that his character wasn't going to get it up for this guy. He was making a choice 'to disdain' and the effect that it was having on me was exactly the effect that it was supposed to be having on my character, which is that I felt impotent.

"DeNiro didn't ever force it. His advice: If they (director/writer) haven't done their job don't force it for them. Let them fix the writing.

"The experience of making a film is an extremely fragmented process. It's hard to get emotionally caught up to a point beyond control.

"You have to be careful when you are writing or directing. It's schizophrenic if you then step in as an actor.

"Very good actors should have a sense of the drama and arc of the piece but on the day of working an actor is in two different head states. He wants to be more in his gut than in his head.

"Writers sometimes don't trust actors and they overwrite. Silence can say a lot.

"One can convey an enormous amount wordlessly. Different from the theatre."

Liv Ullman: Excerpts from <u>Reel Pieces</u>

"Ingmar Bergman didn't rehearse except for <u>Scenes from a Marriage</u>.

"I like to do one or two takes. More are shot but keep the first take. Kubrick would do 60 takes and I would relax for 40 of them.

"Unlike film, in the theatre you know where you are all the time as you keep the whole play in your head.

"I am too impatient to work with bad directors who are doing their home-work on you or don't know what they're doing. It's boring.

"You must make the actors feel really safe so they can do their best work."

Morgan Freeman: From <u>Inside the Actors Studio</u> on BRAVO

"What do I want from a director? Get out of the way. What do I not want? Direction."

Alec Baldwin: From <u>Reel Pieces</u>

"Every actor, no matter how good, needs a director."

Frances McDormand: Excerpts from <u>Reel Pieces</u>

"The experiences that I've had that have been the most satisfying are with the directors who are clearly in control of what they're doing.

"The difference between working in theatre and working in film—(in film) much more energy is put towards waiting and then trying to put out in dynamic spurts—trying to maintain the energy.

"When I work with directors who have a really solid idea of what the arc of the character and the story is then I think that the work I do is consistent. Generally my work isn't consistent because I'm still learning how to do it. In the theatre you gain control of the character during the rehearsal process and then you can maintain that."

Robert Redford: Excerpts from <u>Reel Pieces</u>

"I like improvisation. I do encourage it at times. But it shouldn't be seen. It should be seamless.

"Actors' courage should be honored. Actors should be cared for. See where they want to go, then cut all the fat. It's a process of refinement.

"Georgia O'Keefe said 'there's nothing less real than realism. It's only by the process of selection, elimination and emphasis that you can get to the true meaning of something.' That says a lot about the way I feel about acting."

Annette Bening: Excerpts from <u>Reel Pieces</u>

"I think that a director is your ally and a director who is great makes you feel as though they have as much invested emotionally in the performance as you do. They are also your greatest audience and they are your truth teller as well. So if there's a problem, someone is there to say it, because we've all seen movies where we thought 'Why didn't someone say something?' and as an actor you're very vulnerable. You need that. You need someone to say 'more' or 'less.' Or it might be something very technical.

"The philosophy of Istvan Szabo (director of <u>Being Julia</u>, 2004) is to follow the actor so it's not about anything else other than what's going on between the people. It's not about trying to make fancy shots.

"The directors I've worked with don't say a lot once they've cast you. They stay out of your way. They just love you, they think you're marvelous, they're fascinated by you, they're entertained by you. They love what you do. They make you feel sufficient. They make you feel like 'I've done enough!' "

As I did this research I was again struck by the intelligence, seriousness of purpose, and articulate expression of these actors in regard to their craft. As a rule, actors don't like to talk about how they do what they do. They tend to keep it to themselves. Although film actors are most often contractually required to do specific personal appearances (called p.a.'s) to promote the opening of a current project, the purpose is to charm their audience and sell the picture so we rarely hear about craft. And we are inclined to think of them in the persona of whatever role they might currently be playing. One doesn't often get an opportunity to learn about what they are really feeling and thinking. In working with their directors, most of the exchange deals with the realization of the role at hand and it is rare that there might be either the time or the desire to share their thoughts beyond present business.

The more you can learn about the actor the more skillfully you will be able to play that actor's instrument. Years ago I was fortunate enough to be included in one of the first small groups of grantees as part of the Directing Workshop for Women of the

American Film Institute. We were, in the days when the opportunities for female feature film directors were nonexistent, given the means to shoot short films along with the accompanying exposure, which might result in our entry into the film community. The women who were chosen had, for the most part, already gained acclaim as actors, writers, and/or theatre directors and I was honored to be in their company.

At one of our regular meetings to share experiences and compare notes, one of us (a celebrated lyricist/composer) told us about something unexpected that had occurred. She had managed to get the consent of a very well-known star to play the lead role in her short script and she had asked this actor if she would be willing to meet for breakfast at her home and discuss the script and the role. The actor readily agreed and showed up at the director's home bright and early. Over coffee and bagels the actor talked about herself: her history, her traumas, her triumphs, her loves, her origins, and so on for several hours. Then she rose from the table exclaiming "This was great! Thanks so much. I'm looking forward to it." She then picked up her things and quickly left before her rapt listener could recover. Our director colleague was stunned as she realized that they hadn't talked at all about the character or the script. What a disaster, she thought. But then she realized what had taken place. The actor had generously given the director as much information as possible about herself and her instrument, trusting that the director would then be able to select what was needed from that reservoir, enabling her to collaborate with the actor in the creation of the character and the fulfillment of her vision. The story was a great lesson for all present at that meeting.

12

Tips for the Director

As I write this chapter we happen to be on the verge of another spring awards season. Celebrations, such as the Oscars (Academy of Motion Picture Arts and Sciences), the DGA awards (Directors Guild of America), the People's Choice Awards (Foreign Press Association), the Tonys (Broadway production), and the Obies (Off-Broadway production), which mainly have to do with the economics of our business, abound. I was startled to read an article that announced that this year—2005—the average age of the five directors nominated for the Best Director category by the Academy was sixty. And yet why was I surprised? It takes a long time and a lot of doing it to get to the point where one can really do it well. This craft can't be mastered simply by reading about it. It takes constant exploration, experimentation, trial and error, and interaction with many different actors to develop the necessary skills required for this aspect of the work. In the old days, the bromide was "I've got a barn, let's put on a show." Today it is more apt to be "I've got a camera, let's shoot a film." This accessibility does not necessarily make for skilled results or great filmmaking.

Although there is an ever-growing supply of film product, (much of it of questionable quality); the theatre currently suffers a paucity of straight plays (as opposed to imported musicals) and new dramatists, leaving a large gap waiting to be filled. Although I am sure that there are many gifted and determined playwrights toiling away throughout the United States, the current economics involved in launching anything more than a staged reading is so daunting that few producers are willing to take a chance on the new and untried. However, the determined continue to pursue their dreams in workshops, off-off-Broadway projects, and countless small theatre groups, which offer the opportunity to hone the craft of directing as well as the possibility of instant gratification in the presence of an often much more dedicated and sometimes even more forgiving audience. Therefore *I often urge my film students to use the theatre as a means to get this most necessary experience in working with actors.* Just as I think of the throughline of your script as a journey, so do I think of the quest for skill as a director of actors as a similar mountain climb. Here are some tips that might help ease passage through the crevices and crannies along the way.

NECESSARY ATTRIBUTES

One of the most important attributes of the successful director is **PATIENCE**. The desire to get what you want, to see it immediately, is like the addict's need for a drug and is equally destructive to the process. Actors work gradually, adding a layer at a time. Pushing them to deliver or show you a finished character before the preparation has been completed will most often give you a one-dimensional result that is flat and unsatisfying. It may force you into panicky tampering with the choices in an attempt to make adjustments. This can, at best, often lead to confusion and, at worst, engender hostility on the part of the actors who know that what they need is time to do the work.

I sometimes use the metaphor of baking the chocolate cake in talking to my classes: You are the baker and you gather the necessary ingredients to produce the chocolate, cake, i.e., flour, butter, sugar, baking soda, eggs, chocolate, and so on. You combine these ingredients in the proper amounts and put them in the oven to bake. Each individual ingredient knows what it is supposed to do and does it in relation to the others. However, that's really all they know. You are the only one who knows what that cake is going to look like when it comes out of the oven. But you must let the ingredients do their thing as the baking takes place. And you must wait the appropriate amount of time for it to be finished. Hopefully, when it emerges from the oven, that cake will present itself as complete and be just what you envisioned.

This topic of the layering process that an actor goes through leads me to another thought: I've always felt that *the talent of a director of actors lies in knowing when to give the next direction.* You may feel that this is an instinct that one is either born with or not, but I believe it is an instinct that can be developed over time, honed by each new experience with each different actor. The actor must be allowed to absorb and synthesize what has been suggested in a given rehearsal as part of his homework before he/she is ready to take on additional direction. Because each actor's processing equipment is different, the time frame is also different. Some actors work slowly at the beginning and flower suddenly. Others seem to be able to comprehend and absorb a direction almost immediately. Although sometimes this time frame is in relation to the nature of their training, it has nothing to do with their ability as actors. As directors it is up to us to develop that special sensitivity to the rhythms and needs of our actors.

Another important attribute for the successful director is **PUNCTUALITY**. Ideally *you should be the first one on the set or in the rehearsal hall.* I can't stress how important this is, particularly in terms of your relationships with your actors. Remember, trust is one of the most important components in the working relationship. The actors' trust in you as their leader is immediately frayed by the lack of respect shown by tardiness. When an actor has busted his backside to get there on time prepared to work and finds him/herself munching doughnuts at the craft table awaiting your arrival, you are letting yourself in for impatience, hostility, and all sorts of other negative feelings.

Unfortunately, this ability to get to a place on time is not engendered in our current culture. We seem to live in an "I–me" period where regard for our fellow man is at best secondary. We shove our ways in and out of buses and subway cars, we seem to place little value on commitment if something better comes along, we can't take the time to write a thank-you note (expect an email at best!), and we shout at each other in cars if we feel so inclined. All in all, if only as self-protection, we are being trained to look after number one even if it has to be at the expense of others.

The mind set that must be created to foster ongoing punctuality seems to rely solely on the persistence of a parent attempting to shape a child's life habits. If the parent doesn't have this trait, how will that parent be expected to pass it along to the child? Even in an academic setting I have noted with dismay that there seems to be little regard for the clock. Many professors arrive late to classes as do their students. While this is not particularly important to the teaching of history or economics or even various forms of writing as long as the duration of the class fulfills requirements, I feel it is

disastrous for directing classes. In fact, I have often been so tyran-
nical as to lock the doors of my classrooms a few minutes after the
appointed hour in the hopes of so embarrassing the student who
must knock to gain entry that he/she thinks twice about coming
late again. If you think I'm harping unduly on a lesser flaw, think
again. *I firmly believe that the consistent lateness of a director can do serious damage to his/her relationship to the team as well as to the budget and
the project as a whole.*

Another particularly necessary attribute for the film director
is **ENDURANCE**. Some would call it stamina. The director is often
called upon to be an intellectual, emotional, and physical athlete.
On any given day and at any given time whether it be theatre or
film, we are bombarded with questions demanding immediate
answers: Is this costume too bulky? Do you need a master shot in
this scene? Can I carry this prop in on my entrance? What do you
think about a filter for this shot? Do you want us to fade the lights
down entirely at the end of this scene? We can't get the convertible
for the shot so is it okay if we shoot through the windshield? There
will be a million different questions demanding quick answers.
And these questions are likely to come in the middle of the
rehearsal process when your attention is on the actors and a thousand other things. Needless to say, an agile mind is required.

There will be days when everything seems to be going wrong.
Your leading man is misbehaving, or your assistant director is
down with the flu, or there is suddenly no heat in the rehearsal hall
on an icy winter day, or you are plagued with massive equipment
failure. You want to sit down in a corner and weep or run home
and suck your thumb, but you must control your feelings and put
on a serene face to preserve the morale of the team and continue to
get the best from your actors. It is all doubly difficult when you are
in a constant state of exhaustion from the huge physical demand
that is often part of the daily routine, particularly when you are on
location for a film shoot or mounting a large musical production.
So while you are trying to put the best possible face on for the sake
of the actors' sense of security, you are also possibly fighting the
physical fatigue engendered by the necessity of being on your feet
for endless hours at a time. Remember, often the rehearsal or the
day's shooting may end but your work may continue into the night
with next day planning, and storyboarding, or rewrites, or dailies.

To cope with these demands, my best advice is to *behave like an
athlete.* Part of your preproduction preparation should include

getting yourself into the best possible physical shape with diet, exercise, or whatever it takes. The most important component of this fitness preparation, and the one most often omitted (especially by film students), is sleep. The combined elements of anxiety, tension, excitement, and work load conspire to rob the director of sufficient amounts of sleep. Lack of sleep tends to lead one toward negative choices as substitutes such as pills, coffee overload, alcohol, drugs, or worse. A word to the wise should be sufficient. You owe it to yourself and your team to get yourself into shape and to get enough sleep. Your actors will need you to be at your sharpest, most perceptive, sensitive, and compassionate, which is an impossible order when you are sleep deprived.

PERSISTENCE, which is defined in my dictionary as "holding firmly and steadfastly to some purpose or undertaking despite obstacles, warnings or setbacks" is yet another important attribute of the director. There are many stories about directors who have nurtured dream projects for sometimes as much as 10 years as they attempted to get the polished script or the necessary funding or the right cast for the realization of the dream. Since directors are confronted with obstacles too numerous to mention and from every quarter on a daily basis, it is necessary to develop a kind of "dog with a bone" mentality. If you really believe in what you're doing, you must develop the patience, fortitude, and strength of conviction that will allow you to stay with it and get through it. This is why I suggest that you don't accept or begin a project unless you really believe in it and are prepared to give it your all.

By the same token, *never surrender to the negative*, or at least not without a fight. If something is worth asking for, then it's worth demanding or even fighting for. Often I hear my students, as they enter the classroom where we are gathered to work on scenes, saying "Oh, it's so hot in here! It's awful!" And then they sit down and sweat. No one thinks of going to the window and opening it or calling maintenance to turn up the air conditioning. They submit to the negative condition of the overheated room. This is inevitably followed by a lecture from me on the necessity of developing a resistance to submission. If it's in your way, get rid of it. If it's broken, get it fixed. If they tell you that you can't have something or someone, i.e., an actor, a prop, a piece of a costume, or a lighting effect, because it's too costly or they just don't have it around, make them get what you want or figure something out that costs less. It is to your best interest and the best interest of the project to fight for what you believe you need or want. This is particularly true regarding the selection of final casting choices as well as in matters concerning the comfort of your actors.

TO COMPROMISE OR NOT TO COMPROMISE

This leads me to another consideration that seems to be an integral part of our work, It is sometimes known as "the big C." The word **COMPROMISE**, which usually has a negative connotation, often rears its head. It is important to understand its implications and know when to refuse and when to accept it. Sometimes for the good of the whole group, the good of the project, or the protection of your dream and/or your health it is necessary to make the compromise.

But there are also instances where compromise might impact so negatively as to be destructive to the result. This is an area in which you will find yourself alone. You are the only one who can make the choice or decide how far you are willing to go to resist the compromise or how much of a compromise you are willing to make.

For example, let us say you have been offered an assignment directing a Broadway play (your first, and every stage director's dream). The play is good and you believe in it deeply, but the producer demands that the deal must include the casting of his wife in the lead role. You know that the actor is not up to the demand of the part and that you have thought of several other talented people who would be infinitely better. Is the opportunity to direct on Broadway worth the compromise of casting an actor whose work might reflect poorly on you and kill a chance for success? Should you say no to the project and wait for the right circumstance where your choices prevail? You are the only person who can answer these questions.

Therefore you must be sure of who you are, what you want, and what your priorities are in order to be able to make a constructive decision. Is it indeed a question of "this above all, to thine own self be true," as Shakespeare's players instruct? How much of your principle, taste, or choice are you willing to compromise? Ours is a tough, unforgiving business and you will be constantly challenged. My warning therefore is "this above all, know thyself!" Then you might be able to decide when and how to make the compromise or when to hold on to your conviction and say no.

What if the content of the play or screenplay supports a concept that is in opposition to your own moral or social or political beliefs? Do you make the compromise and accept the job because your rent is due or your children's school tuition must be paid? Can you make yourself believe in the project sufficiently to be able to bring the best of yourself to it? Too often I see directors agreeing to do projects that contain material they can't support and then attempting to alter or rewrite in such a way as to be able to live with it. This is a dangerous route to travel, filled with traps and pitfalls along the way. To me, it is like trying to give a nose job to an elephant. The results can be disastrous, so I would advise that you wait for the right script or perhaps even write one yourself.

ADDITIONAL ATTRIBUTES

One of the most important assets the director possesses is his/her **INTUITION**. And yet how often do our insecurities make us ignore our intuition and replace an intuitive choice with a more studied and possibly less useful one? Time after time, after listening to my comment about a particular choice in a scene, I hear a student say, "Well, that was my first thought but then I changed it." It is understandably difficult to trust one's instincts completely when one is in the learning stage. It is equally difficult when one is a mature artist being pulled in several directions by other members of a team or one's own indecisiveness. Perhaps one never reaches that point of total security where one can trust one's own intuition without reservation. My feeling is that your instinct is the best friend you've got and if it leads you to an intuitive choice, don't reject the impulse without giving it a shot. By the same token, trust the instincts of your actors. Watch them like hawks and try to read the cues that tell you where their instincts are taking them. Allow that observation to be your guide and if you see something interesting, give that actor permission to follow his/her instinct if necessary. Do not allow yourself to be constrained by a preconceived plan when something happens as a result of the instinct of the moment.

That thought brings us to another important word: **FLEXIBILITY**. Remember that when it comes to human behavior, nothing is written in stone. You may have done all your homework, prepared beautifully, and are ready to start the work with the actors, secure in the knowledge that your blueprint will guide you. But you must allow for the changes, adjustments, and surprises that are part and parcel of the collaborative process and the human condition. That is why I always advise my students to do everything in pencil, never ink. Although it is important to develop your vision and to construct a solid throughline that can guide you through the process, the realization of that vision in collaboration with your team demands that you allow each member to contribute the best of themselves and you must remain flexible enough to entertain that creativity. However, let me interject a word of caution here. Do not mistake my constant reference to collaboration as group direction or group writing. The input and ideas offered by your team must always be examined and accepted or rejected in light of your vision and your throughline. Do not cross the fine line and allow your actors to take over directing and beware of allowing the actors to do too much creative writing during the rehearsal process.

Perhaps the most important piece of advice I can offer is that to be a good director and/or filmmaker it is essential to pursue continued **PERSONAL GROWTH** in an ongoing way. I have already referred to the necessity of intensive research in the preparation of a specific play or screenplay. In addition, if we are to be communicators, interpreters, and storytellers, I believe we must constantly expand our awareness of the world around us, of the issues that confront us, and of the changing social, political, and cultural climate. We must push ourselves beyond the second-hand information received through the various media and attempt to broaden our own direct experience of life and true human behavior under all possible circumstances. Do not assume that you understand the complexities of the emergency room of a hospital or a trial courtroom simply because you've watched ER or Law and Order on television.

Equally important is the necessity of familiarizing oneself with the legacy of our art. That demands the reading of the works of the great playwrights of the past as well as the present (Sheridan, Congreve, Wilde, Synge, O'Casey and O'Neill in addition to Williams, Inge, Anderson, Miller, etc.) and the viewing of the work of our past great film directors (Renoir, Capra, Sturges, Wilder, Keislowski, Welles, etc.). It is not only important for your understanding of the history of the craft, it is also a classroom filled with the innovations and skills of your predecessors. I am always impressed when I listen to Martin Scorcese, the inveterate student of film, run through a list of film greats that he's "stolen" from (his word) when he talks about the making of his most recent project. What he's really saying is that he is learning from the past. I was startled when I discovered that no one in my recent class of graduate film students had ever seen Orson Welles' classic, <u>Citizen Kane</u>. To me it was tantamount to being told by physics majors that they'd never heard of Einstein. *The reservoir of knowledge gained by delving into the history of one's craft becomes the source of food for the creative process and therefore should be an ongoing pursuit.*

Our work as directors is so dynamic that *the only rule that applies is that there are no rules.* What I have presented in this book is only one way of approaching the craft of directing actors. It should be regarded as a possible beginning, as the development of this craft can be a never-ending pursuit. There are, I'm sure, many other methods perhaps equally efficient, equally effective. Finding your own approach to the work is a matter of studying, experimenting, and selecting. You must find the way or ways to do the work that will specifically fit you and your needs. Perhaps you will choose elements of my approach and couple them with elements of others. In the last analysis, whatever works for you and gets the job done is useful.

The thing that makes our work as directors so fascinating is that it is, like human behavior, ever changing, challenging in its infinite variety, exciting, surprising, and often daunting. If we are successful it has the potential of producing, in collaboration with our actors and other members of the team, a piece of creativity that contributes to our culture and is in some way life enhancing. It can be a long, hard journey, but the satisfaction and fulfillment that await are well worth the trip.

Appendix A: Additional Exercises for Workshop or Classroom

REPETITION EXERCISE

Take two actors and assign the same line of dialogue to each actor. The sentence should be complete and simple, i.e., "I really like the snow," or "Did you get here on the subway?" or "You're wearing that suit again." Each actor will continue to say the same line, but with the action that responds to the action the other actor has just pursued. The group watching, armed with pencil and paper and making a column for each actor, will try to identify and write the instinctive action choices as the actors are making them. Select the actor who will start and caution the pair to take time to react to the action received before they respond. The exercise might look something like:

Actor 1: I really like the snow. (Action: to savor)
Actor 2: I really like the snow. (Action: to reject and walks away)
Actor 1: I really like the snow. (Action: to taunt, going after Actor 2)
Actor 2: I really like the snow. (Action: to confront, spinning around to face Actor 1)
Actor 1: I really like the snow! (Action: to challenge)
Actor 2: I really like the snow! (Action: to threaten) and so on.

The necessity of attempting to identify the actors' instinctive choices, which often go by very rapidly, will serve to sharpen the director's perception and assist in the labeling process during the rehearsal period.

THE TELEPHONE GAME

Line the group up in a row or in a semicircle. The person sitting at one end will start by pursuing an action to the person on his or her right without any dialogue or sound. Instead of responding to that person, person number 2 will pursue the responding action to the person on his or her right. Person number 3 will respond to person number 2, but will pursue the responding action to person number 4. And so on down the line. The last person will pursue the responding action to the first person. No dialogue or sound should be allowed throughout the exercise. At the end, the group will review and attempt to identify the action choices starting at number 1 and proceeding down the line.

This exercise helps define and identify doable action verbs and reveals the necessity of pursuing each action as fully and specifically as possible so that the respondent knows how to react.

THE QUICK COLLABORATION EXERCISE

Ask for volunteers from the group for each exercise. First, you will need one writer and one director. The writer must "write" (think up) a situation, location, and two or three characters. It should be kept simple (e.g., two people meet in a dentist's waiting room and discover that they are long lost relatives) and able to be cast from the group. The writer is given 5 minutes for this task. The writer then tells only the director the story and together they select a cast from the group. The director then has 10 minutes in which to give the actors the basic facts of the story and its characters and select life needs and scene needs with them, perhaps with the assistance of the writer. The actors then improvise a scene for the group with the given needs, location, and story elements.

The challenge for the director is to provide the actors with needs that will create obstacles or conflict and give the scene an arc while hopefully realizing the writer's story. At the end of the improvisation, which may have to be stopped by the teacher or leader of the group after a given amount of time, the writer comments on the extent to which the story was realized and the group attempts to identify the needs chosen and comments on that which the team has attempted to communicate. This exercise is designed to strengthen the muscles of collaboration under the stress of time and to force the director to communicate with the actors specifically, cutting away all extraneous talk. Therefore the time constraints must be observed.

THE MARAT SADE EXERCISE

The teacher or director of the group privately assigns each member of the group a need, thereby creating a character other than the member's persona. Members enter the playing space one at a time when pointed at by the director, pursuing the need but without any dialogue of any kind. Once in the playing space, members remain, continuing to pursue their needs as each new member is added, until the entire group is in the playing space pursuing their needs either by themselves or interacting with the others and only the director remains outside. The director has the option of allowing the members to make sounds, as long as they do not talk. The director should allow time for interaction in the playing space each time the next member is invited in.

The success of the exercise relies on the ability of the leader to assign potentially interesting, interactive, and opposing needs among the members. Since one of the ways to arrive at insanity is to remove the spine or life need of a character and only play the moment-to-moment want of the scene, the assembled group in this exercise often looks like a scene from the play Marat Sade, which takes place in an insane asylum, thus the name of the exercise. In addition to the challenge to the teacher or director to come up with interesting needs choices, the challenge to a participant is to find ways to continue to pursue the assigned need without dialogue over an extended period of time while continuing to interact with others. At the end of the exercise the group discusses and attempts to identify the needs choices in the order in which each member entered the playing space.

THE IMPROVISATION ROUND

The teacher or director privately assigns a complete character outline—life need and scene need—to each member of the group and selects a member to start the round. Actor 1 decides on the scene, i.e., environment, and finds a way to share that information with Actor 2 as he/she enters the scene upon a tap from the teacher/director. Actors 1 and 2, using dialogue and pursuing their needs, improvise the ensuing scene until they hear a single hand clap from the teacher/director. Actor 1 finds a way to leave the scene. The teacher/director taps Actor 3, who enters the scene. Actor 2 can either remain in the same environment or change it, once again, finding a way to inform Actor 3 as to where they are. Actors 2 and 3 improvise their scene until they hear the clap from the teacher/director. Actor 2 leaves the scene and the teacher/director taps Actor 4, who then plays with Actor 3 and so on until all the members have had a chance to participate.

The time allowed for each two-person segment is at the discretion of the teacher/director and depends on the size of the group and the content and fulfillment of each improvisation, but it should not be allowed to go on indefinitely. At the end of the exercise the group discusses and attempts to identify the needs choices made by the teacher/director for each character, starting with Actor 1. This exercise demands some skill on the part of the teacher/director in timing the choice of each participant, based on his/her knowledge of the assigned character outline. If, for example, one were to call in the *win her in order to prove manhood* character to join the *get approval in order to get love* character, there wouldn't be much of a scene as the two characters would get together very quickly. But if the *win her in order to prove manhood* character joined the *prove womanhood in order to free herself* character, there would certainly be a chance for tension and an arc. For the participants, this exercise demands focus and concentration on the character outline, as well as fast, clear thinking and the use of both dialogue and surroundings to pursue the needs.

ACTION LABELING EXERCISE

This is an exercise designed to enable the film director to identify actors' action choices as they occur on a moment-to-moment basis. Obtain a tape or DVD of a film that is small canvas, character based rather than action based, such as the 2005 Oscar-nominated Sideways or the 1934 period piece, It Happened One Night. Get together a small group and review the film in its entirety and then discuss the possible throughline and life needs of the principal characters. Select a two-character scene in the film to view again and try to identify the scene needs of each character. Then, using the pause button on your remote when necessary, try to identify the moment-to-moment action choices of each actor. Since in this finished product the needs and actions are synthesized to the point where they appear to be and sometimes are instinctive, it takes a sharpened eye to be able to deconstruct the behavioral choice.

We have found in my Workshop that the inclusion and active participation of actors, writers, and directors in all of the exercises described here prove to be equally useful for all disciplines. In addition to providing a means to understanding the approach and sharpening the vocabulary, I think you will find that they're a lot of fun!

Appendix B: Suggested Reading and Viewing

The following book and film titles are suggested specifically for their usefulness in studying the actor's craft, the director–actor collaborative process, and some of the literature of our art from both the past and the present.

READING

Respect for Acting by Uta Hagen
A Challenge to the Actor by Uta Hagen
Sanford Meisner on Acting by Sanford Meisner and Dennis Longwell
The Technique of Acting by Stella Adler
A Dream of Passion: The Development of the Method by Lee Strasberg
An Actor Prepares by Constantin Stanislavski
Building a Character by Constantin Stanislavski
Creating a Role by Constantin Stanislavski
Making Movies by Sidney Lumet
On Directing by Harold Clurman
Arthur Miller's Collected Plays
A Streetcar Named Desire by Tennessee Williams
Glass Menagerie by Tennessee Williams
Cat on a Hot Tin Roof by Tennessee Williams

VIEWING

Ordinary People 1980 Robert Redford, director
A Streetcar Named Desire 1951 Elia Kazan, director
On the Waterfront 1954 Elia Kazan, director
Tootsie 1982 Sidney Pollock, director
One-Eyed Jacks 1961 Marlon Brando, director
Chinatown 1974 Roman Polanski, director
Citizen Kane 1941 Orson Welles, director
All About Eve 1950 Joseph L. Mankiewicz, director
East of Eden 1955 Elia Kazan, director
The Ice Storm 1997 Ang Lee, director
Sense and Sensibility 1995 Ang Lee, director
The Fast Runner 2001 Zacharias Kunuk, director
The Motorcycle Diaries 2004 Walter Salles, director
Rebel Without a Cause 1955 Nicholas Ray, director
The Treasure of Sierra Madre 1948 John Huston, director
Brokeback Mountain 2005 Ang Lee, director
The Decalogue 1988 Krzysztof Kieslowski, director
Three Colors: Red 1994 Krzysztof Kieslowski, director
400 Blows 1959 Francois Truffaut, director
Boys Don't Cry 1999 Kim Peirce, director

Glossary

A method: Any *modus operandi*, technique, or process developed by the individual actor that will assist in the work of the actor.

Actions: Psychological, subtextual *doings* expressed in actable verbs that motivate behavior on a moment-to-moment basis and that are pursued in order to accomplish the continuing pursuit of the scene need.

Activity: The physical movement involved in the accomplishment of work, tasks, exercise, amusement etc., such as ironing a shirt, combing one's hair, or typing at a computer.

AD: Assistant Director

Antagonist: The character who stands in the way of the forward motion of the throughline and/or prevents or impedes the protagonist's journey to the conclusion.

Beat: A segment of a scene, much like a musical phrase, ending when the subject matter changes, or there is an entrance or exit, or the scene takes another direction.

Coverage: The filming of a shot or beat from as many angles or in as many ways as time and budget will allow so as to provide ample choice in the editing phase of the work.

DP: Director of Photography

Emotional Memory: An exercise in which the recall of sensory detail associated with an experience of a specific emotion is used to recreate an emotional state such as grief, anger, joy, despair, etc. Can also be used as a preparation.

Flatliner: A play or screenplay lacking in structure or written in a stream-of-consciousness style that is further compounded by the director's lack of structure and/or construction of an arc.

185

Givens: Any and all specific information appearing in the text that can be useful in constructing the back story, characteristics, and behavior of a character.

Jump ball: The action choices for each actor at the very beginning of each scene that are designed to start the give and take in the moment-to-moment pursuit of scene needs.

Life Need: The underlying, subtextual want or drive or goal of the character that is present and pursued from the very beginning of the script until the very end.

Organic connection: Gut-level truth in reflexive reaction that the actor seeks in finding the behavior of the character.

Outline: The life need and scene need choices that provide the bone structure of a character.

Personalization: The process by which an actor might connect to the need or emotional demand of the character or scene by substituting his/her own personal experience or specific individual as part of the preparation.

Practical: Anything that is functional and works well. Originally used in the theatre to define that which was real on a set as opposed to a set piece or that which was painted, as in a door that opens and closes or a sink that has running water.

Preparation: The process by which an actor readies him/herself to fulfill the emotional and motivational demands of the character at the beginning of the scene or shot.

Protagonist: The character who carries the throughline forward and takes the journey to its conclusion.

Scene Need: The underlying, subtextual immediate want or drive or goal of the character in each scene that is pursued in order to accomplish the continued pursuit of the life need.

Sense Memory: An exercise in which the sensory detail involved in a task or state of being is recalled minutely, enabling the actor to recreate the total experience organically.

State of Being: Physical states such as heat, cold, illness, pain, disability, etc.

Storyboards: A pictorial representation of the shot-by-shot plan by means of a series of sketches laid out in panels that define what the camera will see.

The Method: A technique originally advanced by Constantin Stanislavski that was designed to enable the actor to create a character organically, which was translated and developed further in the United States by Stella Adler, Lee Strasberg, and many other disciples.

Throughline: The main idea or statement that the director wants to communicate to the audience or have the viewers thinking about as they leave the theatre, expressed specifically and concisely in a sentence or two and developed in the journey through the narrative.

INDEX

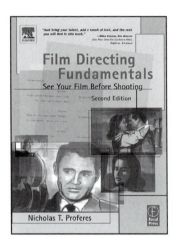